# WALKS IN NATURE

## AUSTRALIA

**EXPLORE**
**AUSTRALIA**

*viola design*

**BUSH HERITAGE**
AUSTRALIA

*Our heart & soul*

10% of Viola Design's profits from the sale of this book go towards Bush Heritage Australia's work protecting Australia's unique animals, plants and their habitats.

# CONTENTS

## SYDNEY

## CANBERRA

## MELBOURNE

## ADELAIDE

# WALKS IN NATURE
## AUSTRALIA

*Walks in Nature: Australia* is a celebration of being outdoors. From the country's elegant eastern sweep to its western shore and south to the Apple Isle, there's a bounty of easily accessible walking trails all around the country.

We've scoured the country in search of the very best and they're all included here: 112 incredible walks that'll have you escaping into nature; climbing mountains, exploring ancient rainforests, dropping into hidden valleys, swimming with sea turtles, crossing rivers and spotting native animals – all within a two-hour drive from your capital city (Sydney, Canberra, Melbourne, Adelaide, Perth, Brisbane and Hobart).

There is a plethora of urban nature walks on offer too: follow the Brisbane River as it wends through the subtropical city's lush gardens; admire the panoramic views of the City of Churches from the Adelaide Hills; discover the wildlife corridors through Melbourne; and wander under a canopy of wattle in the nation's capital.

As each city's climate and landscape varies considerably, we've suggested the ideal time of year to tackle each walk. In Sydney, for instance, coastal walks promise cool breezes and ocean swimming, inland walks to Indigenous art reflect the hues of autumn, winter chills are warded off by historic carriageways and strenuous Blue Mountains climbs, and walks through swathes of native wildflowers herald the birth of spring.

For each walk there's a clear and detailed map; on the other page there's a photo and easy-to-follow information on what you'll encounter along the way as well as a suggested place to stop for a coffee, a light meal, or to buy delicious local produce.

For some walks you are allowed to take your dog – always carry a leash and obey any signs. In some areas, mobile phone coverage will be limited. Always take something to eat and drink, as some of these walks are quite strenuous, and there may not be any access to drinking water.

So dust off your daypack, pull on your boots, grab your hat and make a beeline for the bush trails that crisscross and surround your city. There's so much to discover on a walk in nature.

# SYDNEY
## NEW SOUTH WALES

Skirted by sea and bordered by the eucalypt-clad walls of the Blue Mountains, the thriving metropolis of Sydney is much more than a centre of business – it's a windfall of unique natural habitats.

You don't need to roam far to find yourself dwarfed by blue gum forests, trekking along sparkling bays, diving into sheltered coves and iconic beachside baths, or admiring spectacular cliff-top panoramas.

Follow the paths around the inner harbour, taking in iconic Sydney sites before seeking out the green patches of national parks that punctuate the suburbs. Here, you'll find corridors of scribbly gums standing sentinel over winding rivers, and a troop of native animals: from possums, swamp wallabies, sugar gliders and echidnas to warbling wattlebirds and brilliantly coloured lorikeets.

To the north and south, great swathes of national park offer walkers respite from the city bustle. The country's oldest national park, the Royal, offers the sublime Coast Track, a two-day hike that we tackle in parts, capped off with a ferry ride or an ocean swim.

Finally, the Blue Mountains National Park is a bushwalkers' paradise. There are cliff-top hikes, strenuous, vertigo-inducing climbs, and serene strolls through stands of statuesque eucalypts to keep you ever coming back for more.

Photo: Hanging Rock at Blackheath, Blue Mountains © Tourism Australia, Sue Wright
Photo: Fresh apples in crates, Blue Mountains © Destination NSW, Hamilton Lund

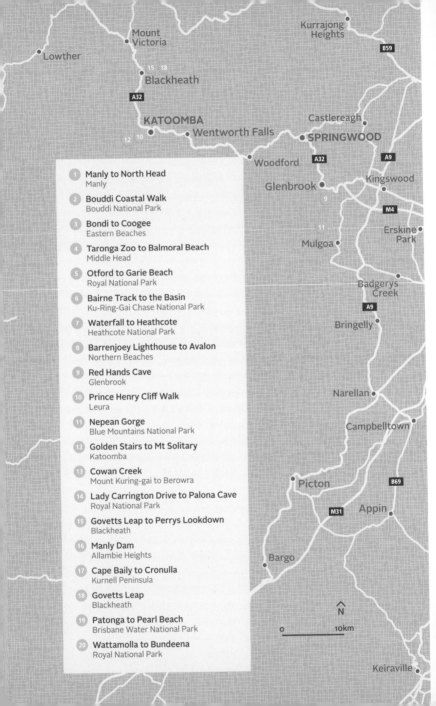

1. **Manly to North Head**
   Manly

2. **Bouddi Coastal Walk**
   Bouddi National Park

3. **Bondi to Coogee**
   Eastern Beaches

4. **Taronga Zoo to Balmoral Beach**
   Middle Head

5. **Otford to Garie Beach**
   Royal National Park

6. **Bairne Track to the Basin**
   Ku-Ring-Gai Chase National Park

7. **Waterfall to Heathcote**
   Heathcote National Park

8. **Barrenjoey Lighthouse to Avalon**
   Northern Beaches

9. **Red Hands Cave**
   Glenbrook

10. **Prince Henry Cliff Walk**
    Leura

11. **Nepean Gorge**
    Blue Mountains National Park

12. **Golden Stairs to Mt Solitary**
    Katoomba

13. **Cowan Creek**
    Mount Kuring-gai to Berowra

14. **Lady Carrington Drive to Palona Cave**
    Royal National Park

15. **Govetts Leap to Perrys Lookdown**
    Blackheath

16. **Manly Dam**
    Allambie Heights

17. **Cape Baily to Cronulla**
    Kurnell Peninsula

18. **Govetts Leap**
    Blackheath

19. **Patonga to Pearl Beach**
    Brisbane Water National Park

20. **Wattamolla to Bundeena**
    Royal National Park

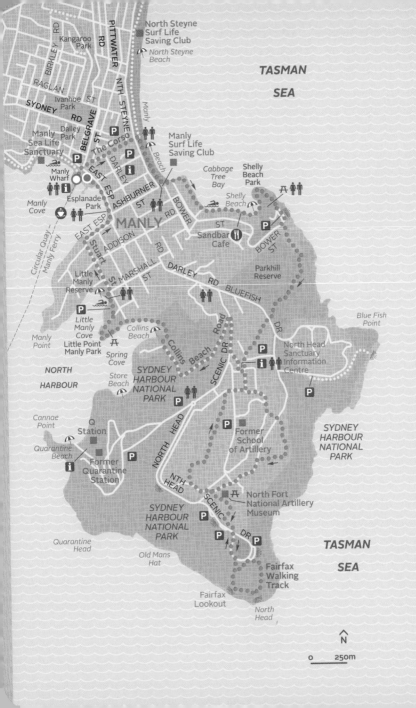

# MANLY TO NORTH HEAD
## MANLY

Scenic circuit walk with ocean vistas, rugged cliff-faces, historic artillery sites and little-known beaches.

From the ferry wharf, walk along the Corso to Manly's sand crescent. Head right along the esplanade before joining the footpath to Shelly Beach. Stop for breakfast at the Sandbar Cafe (Marine Pde), then follow the path around the headland and uphill to the North Head track. Cross Bluefish Dr en route to the former School of Artillery. Join Gunners' Walk past the North Fort National Artillery Museum. Turn left on Scenic Dr and join the Fairfax Walking Track, which provides incredible views of the 90m high cliffs of North Head. Rejoin Gunners' Walk and mosey downhill to Collins Beach. Pick up the track on the far side of the sand before arriving at Little Manly Cove's netted pool. From here, turn left on Stuart St and take the footpath around the water to the wharf.

**Location**
20km north from Sydney

**Distance**
11km circuit

**Grade**
Medium

**Ideal Season**
Summer

**Map**
UBD 198 B10

**Notes**
Track sealed and unsealed
Exposed

Photo: Manly Beach
© Kim Navarre

# BOUDDI COASTAL WALK
## BOUDDI NATIONAL PARK

Coastal walk through heathland and eucalypt
forests taking in spectacular ocean views and
a shipwreck.

At the eastern end of Putty Beach, climb stairs
to a boardwalk that leads to Bullimah Beach
and Gerrin Point Lookout. Enjoy sparkling views
of Maitland Bay, which is a feeding ground for
white-bellied sea eagles and humpback whales.
Continue through woodland and heath to
Maitland Bay Track, which spills onto a beach
that at low tide reveals the rusting remains of the
PS *Maitland* – wrecked in 1898. Follow the track
onto the Bombi Moor, sand dunes dominated by
wallum banksias, and on to Little Beach, ideal
for a swim. From here, the track winds uphill to
the Mourawaring Moor fire trail, before reaching
Beachview Esplanade. Head on to the start of
MacMasters Track, which leads down to the
sand. Drop in at MacMasters Beach Cafe
(61 Marine Pde) for top-notch coffee and
burgers. Return the way you came.

**Location**
98km north from
Sydney

**Distance**
16km return

**Grade**
Medium

**Ideal Season**
Summer

**Map**
UBD
Central Coast
118 C1

**Notes**
No dogs
Track sealed
and unsealed

Photo: Wallum heath in the Bombi Moor
© Doug Beckers

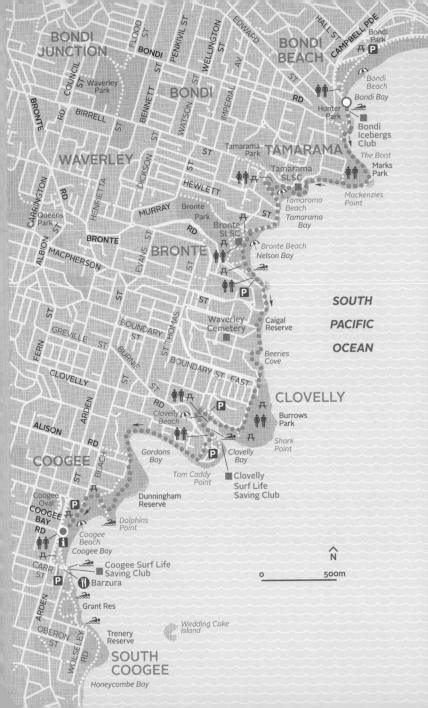

# BONDI TO COOGEE
## EASTERN BEACHES

Sydney's renowned coastal walk skirts dramatic cliff-tops and golden beaches and dips into inviting ocean pools.

From the southern end of Bondi Beach follow the path to Mackenzies Point, with great views over the iconic stretch of sand and southern coastal cliffs. Continue to Tamarama Beach. Cross the park, walk up the stairs and along the pathway to Bronte Beach's popular crescent. Cool off in the ocean bath or under the towering Norfolk Island pines that hug the beach. Rejoin the path as it slides past Waverley Cemetery, the last resting place for famous Aussies such as cricketer Victor Trumper and writer Henry Lawson. Cross Burrows Park before arriving at the deep snorkellers' paradise of Clovelly. Amble around Gordons Bay to the northern headland above Coogee Beach. Take the path down to the sand. Barzura (62 Carr St) has Fairtrade coffee to slake your thirst. Return the way you came.

3

Location
9km east from Sydney

Distance
12km return

Grade
Medium

Ideal Season
Summer

Map
UBD 26 L6

Notes
Track sealed
Exposed
Very busy on weekends

Photo: Tamarama Beach
© Sacha Fernandez

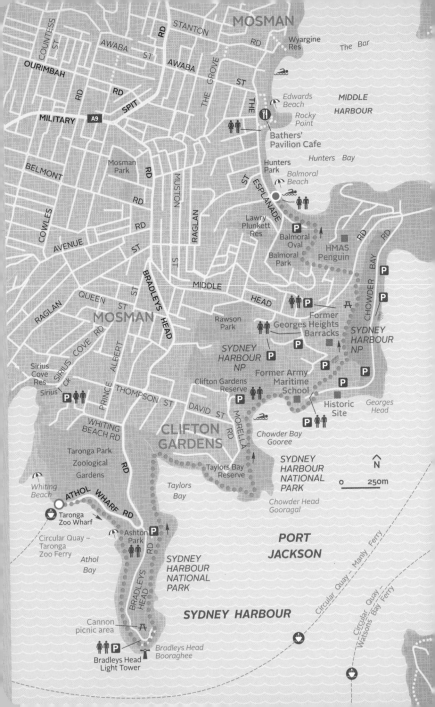

# TARONGA ZOO TO BALMORAL BEACH
## MIDDLE HEAD

Peaceful harbour walk with sublime water views, bushland and beaches, and a stash of exotic animals.

From Taronga Zoo Wharf, walk uphill before joining a pathway that leads into Sydney Harbour National Park. For a quiet dip, follow the Athol Beach track to a patch of sand where the city view is unrivalled. Rejoin the trail and climb steps flanked by Sydney red gums before reaching Bradleys Head. Continue along the path to Taylors Bay, passing through sweetly scented forest, and on to Chowder Bay. Enjoy a dip in the baths and a picnic in Clifton Gardens Reserve. Rejoin the track at the northern end of the beach and go past the former Army Maritime School en route to Georges Heights. Cross Middle Head Rd, climb the stairs to Balmoral Oval and arrive at the beach. Try Mediterranean-style food at the colourful Bathers' Pavilion Cafe (4 The Esplanade). Return the way you came.

Location
13km north-east
from Sydney

Distance
13km return

Grade
Medium

Ideal Season
Summer

Map
UBD 217 A15

Notes
Track unsealed
Shady
Catch a ferry
to Taronga Zoo
Wharf from
Circular Quay

Photo: Giraffe with a city view
© Tourism Australia, Ian Lever

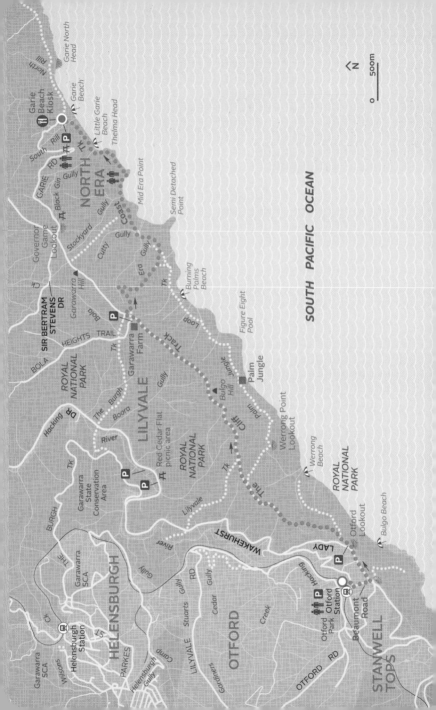

# OTFORD TO GARIE BEACH
## ROYAL NATIONAL PARK

Spectacular coastal walk through pristine rainforest and woodland and along sun-soaked swimming beaches.

Starting at Otford Station, take the overhead bridge and steep stairs to meet a fire trail. Walk along Beaumont Rd to Lady Wakehurst Dr and turn left. Leave the road at Otford Lookout and join the Cliff Track. Continue uphill until the track flattens out and passes through eucalypts and Gymea lilies. At the Garawarra Farm intersection head right along the Garie Beach track through stunted heath, before heading downhill through rainforest and across a hillside of native grass. At Burning Palms take the raised walkway past the surf club and up a track that winds around National Trust beach shacks. Follow the signs to North Era: check out the cave and the spa-like pool. Climb Thelma Head before dropping down to Little Garie then Garie beaches. There's a kiosk at the surf club. Return the way you came.

5

**Location**
60km south from Sydney

**Distance**
19km return

**Grade**
Medium

**Ideal Season**
Summer

**Map**
UBD Wollongong 14 G3

**Notes**
Track unsealed
This is the first section of the Coast Track, a 28km one-way journey from Otford to Bundeena

Sydney

KU-RING-GAI CHASE
LAMBERT PENINSULA
NORTH MACKEREL TK
Mackerel Beach Wharf
Great Mackerel Beach
Palm Beach – Patonga – Bobbin Head Ferry
Ettalong – Palm Beach Ferry
Challenger
Road
Tk
KU-RING-GAI CHASE NATIONAL PARK
Cowan Creek
Basin Aboriginal art site
MACKEREL
TK
GREAT MACKEREL BEACH
Basin
America Bay Tk
Head
Currawong Wharf
Palm Beach – The Basin – Mackerel Beach Ferry
Palm Beach Public Wharf
CURRAWONG BEACH
Euro Tk
Snapperman Beach
BARRENJOEY RD
West
N
Topham Tk
The Basin picnic area
The Basin Wharf
Retreat
Soldiers Point
Coasters
0 500m
The Basin
Bennetts Wharf
PITTWATER
Sand Point
McKay Res
COASTERS RETREAT
Basin Lookout
Bonnie Doon Wharf
RD
HEAD
WEST
Bairne
SOLDIERS POINT TK
PALM BEACH
Portuguese Beach
Portuguese Bay
Careel Bay
Track
Waterfront Store & Cafe 13km
TOWLERS LOOKOUT TRAIL
Portuguese
Tk

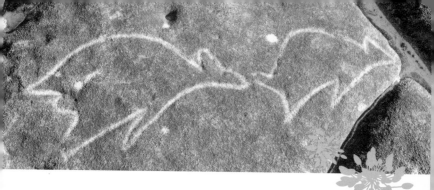

# BAIRNE TRACK TO THE BASIN
## KU-RING-GAI CHASE NATIONAL PARK

Stunning walk along ridge tops to secluded beaches, an enticing lagoon and detailed Indigenous engravings.

From the parking area follow the marked trail through hairpin banksias and feasting honeyeaters, and along a ridge covered with casuarinas. Ignore the Towlers Bay and Soldiers Point tracks to arrive at a lookout with panoramic views over glistening Careel Bay. Retrace your steps to an unsignposted track on your right that zigzags down a hill past rock platforms to Coasters Retreat. Cross the inlet at low tide or, when the water's higher, catch a ferry from Bonnie Doon Wharf. Cool off here before walking up the Basin Track to engravings, including a mob of wallabies and a speared shark. Turn left at West Head Rd and walk to the parking area. Stop at the Waterfront Store & Cafe (1860 Pittwater Rd, Church Point) for over-water dining.

**Location**
45km north from Sydney

**Distance**
11km circuit

**Grade**
Medium

**Ideal Season**
Autumn

**Map**
UBD 97 K5

**Notes**
No dogs
Track unsealed
Includes one of Australia's most well-preserved and significant Indigenous engraving sites

Photo: Basin Track engraving site
© John Finch

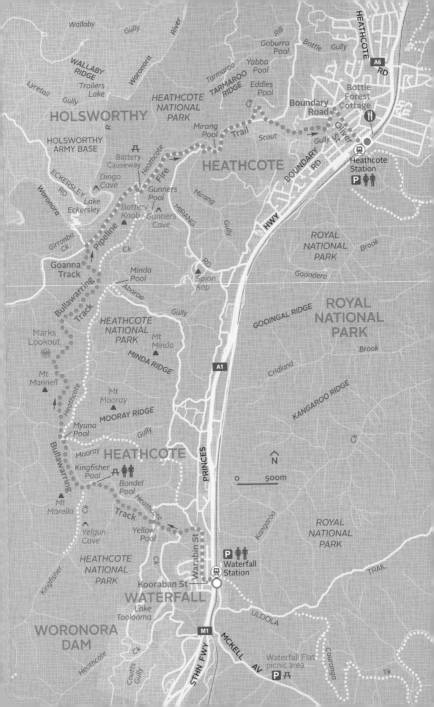

# WATERFALL TO HEATHCOTE
## HEATHCOTE NATIONAL PARK

Challenging walk through rugged, wildflower-strewn Heathcote Valley around waterholes, over boulders and beneath sculptural gums.

From Waterfall Station, cross the bridge over the highway and walk along Kooraban and Warabin sts before taking the Bullawarring Track towards Heathcote. Cross Heathcote Creek and accompany it downstream to Kingfisher Pool, which is a great place for a dip. Beyond the cleared camping area, rejoin the track as it winds between boulders, across Kingfisher Creek and downstream. Following the Battery Causeway signs, head up the ridge, turn left onto Goanna Track and then right onto the pipeline fire trail, which leads to Battery Causeway. Cross Heathcote Creek and continue to Mirang and Eddles pools. Cross a metal footbridge and walk uphill along a narrow track. Take Boundary Rd then Oliver St to the Heathcote Station and Bottle Forest Cottage (1330 Princes Hwy, Heathcote).

**Location**
45km south from Sydney

**Distance**
12km one way

**Grade**
Medium

**Ideal Season**
Autumn

**Map**
UBD 351 Q12

**Notes**
No dogs
Track unsealed
Starts at Waterfall Station; ends at Heathcote Station

Photo: A water gum flower, *Tristaniopsis laurina*, Heathcote National Park
© John Tann

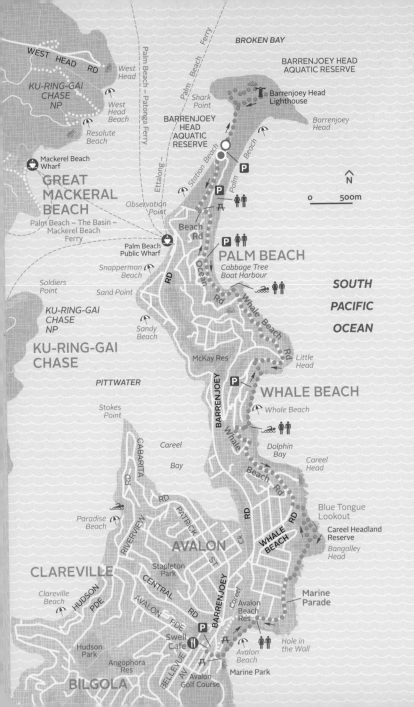

# BARRENJOEY
# LIGHTHOUSE TO AVALON
## NORTHERN BEACHES

8

Spectacular coastal walk on a convict-built track, along idyllic surf beaches and over dramatic headlands.

Walk towards Barrenjoey Head and onto Station Beach. At the northern end of the sand, take Smugglers Track uphill to the stone lighthouse, built in 1881. Return the way you came and follow Beach and Ocean rds to the southern end of Palm Beach. Climb the wooden stairs near the rock baths to Whale Beach Rd and on to Little Head, which has sublime ocean views. Take the stairs down to the sea before climbing stone steps at the southern end of the beach to Malo and Whale Beach rds. Continue to Bangalley Head steps and a loop track that delivers you to the cliff-edge. Walk along the track to Marine Pde and Avalon Beach. Try the cornbread at Swell Cafe (74 Old Barrenjoey Rd) before retracing your steps.

**Location**
45km north from Sydney

**Distance**
20km return

**Grade**
Medium

**Ideal Season**
Autumn

**Map**
UBD 78 P14

**Notes**
Exposed
Track sealed
and unsealed
Lighthouse tours
available Sundays
11am–3pm

Photo: Barrenjoey Lighthouse and Palm Beach
© Suzy Jackson

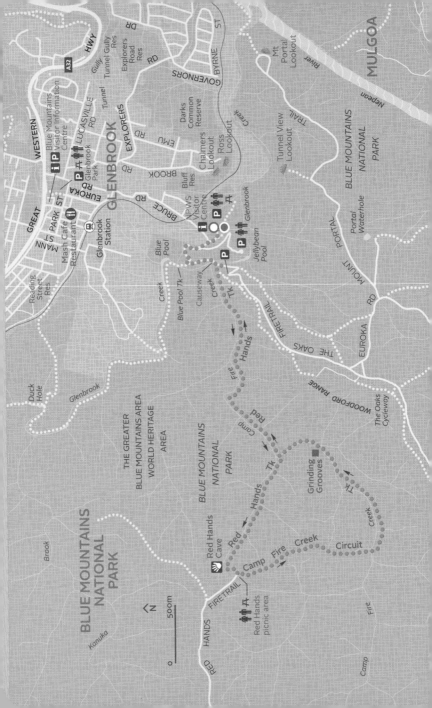

# RED HANDS CAVE
## GLENBROOK

Walk through the eucalypt-and-sandstone Blue
Mountains to some of Sydney's finest Indigenous
hand stencils and axe-grinding grooves.

Starting at the visitor centre, zigzag down the
road to Glenbrook Creek Causeway and take
the track to Red Hands Cave. Follow Camp Fire
Creek through undergrowth to Red Hands Gully
and, after a relaxed 140m climb, to Red Hands
Cave. Discovered by Europeans in 1913, the
cave contains red-ochre hand stencils. Stop for
lunch at Red Hands picnic area before walking
the Camp Fire Creek Circuit down a steep 100m
descent. Look for grinding grooves in sandstone
platforms, as well as water dragons around
the creek. Complete the loop and retrace your
steps to Jellybean Pool where the water's fine for
swimming. Mash Cafe Restaurant (19 Ross St)
serves organic pies and Fairtrade coffee.

9

**Location**
62km west from
Sydney

**Distance**
9km return

**Grade**
Medium

**Ideal Season**
Autumn

**Map**
UBD 181 L5

**Notes**
Track unsealed
Features more
than 50 ochre
hand stencils
of the Daruk
people

Photo: Red Hands Cave
© Dan Riordan

# PRINCE HENRY
# CLIFF WALK
## LEURA

Spectacular Blue Mountains walk with lookouts over sheer escarpments, wooded valleys and cascading waterfalls.

From behind the Scenic Railway and Skyway engine shed, take the concrete path and steps towards Reids Plateau. The cliff-walk veers to the left, passing lookouts above Katoomba Falls. Stop for breakfast at the kiosk here. From the picnic area follow the signs past Katoomba Cascades to Cliff View and Echo Point; the lookouts en route showcase the incredible beauty of the Kedumba Valley and the Blue Mountains' famous rock formation, the Three Sisters. Further on, the panoramas at Honeymoon, Burrabarroo and Jamisons lookouts are magnificent. Tarpeian Rock has incredible views to the valley below while Olympic Rock Lookout is home to rock warblers. Stop for lunch at Gordon Falls Picnic Area before returning the way you came.

**Location**
104km west from Sydney.

**Distance**
16.5km return

**Grade**
Medium

**Ideal Season**
Autumn

**Map**
UBD
Blue Mountains
29 M2

**Notes**
Track sealed and unsealed

Photo: Three Sisters at Echo Point
© Tourism Australia, Lincoln Fowler

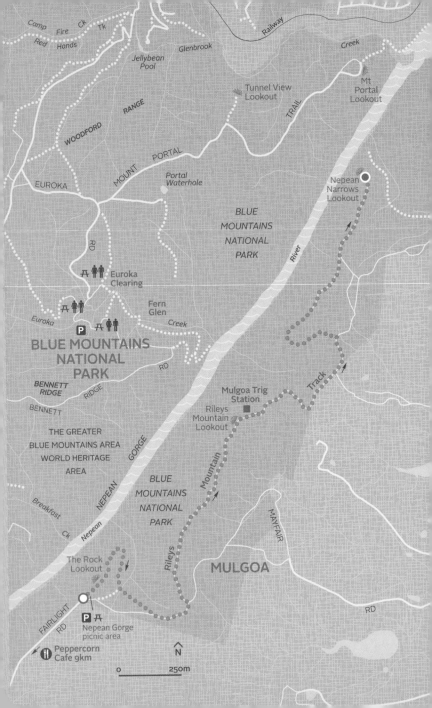

# NEPEAN GORGE
## BLUE MOUNTAINS NATIONAL PARK

Meandering walk through fragrant wattle along quiet fire trails with panoramic views of the Nepean River and Blue Mountains National Park.

From the carpark take the left-hand path just after the Rileys Mountain Lookout sign and head to the Rock Lookout, with sweeping western vistas. Continue along the ridge to another lookout before taking the track due south – don't head down into the gully – where it intersects with a fire trail. Veer left, crossing a ford, and again at the next fire trail intersection. Continue uphill through a young eucalypt forest to Rileys Mountain Lookout and soak up the magnificent panoramas to the tune of bellbirds. Beyond the Mulgoa Trig Station follow a fence line to a locked gate. Roughly 200m on, take the track uphill to the left and 350m later, at a fork, head right on a sandy fire trail along the ridge top. Continue to Nepean Narrows Lookout. Return the way you came. Stop in at Peppercorn Cafe (1319 Mulgoa Rd) for coffee and sweet treats.

11

**Location**
56km west from Sydney

**Distance**
13km return

**Grade**
Medium

**Ideal Season**
Winter

**Map**
UBD 201 K8

**Notes**
No dogs
Track unsealed

Photo: Nepean Gorge
© Rosie Nicolai

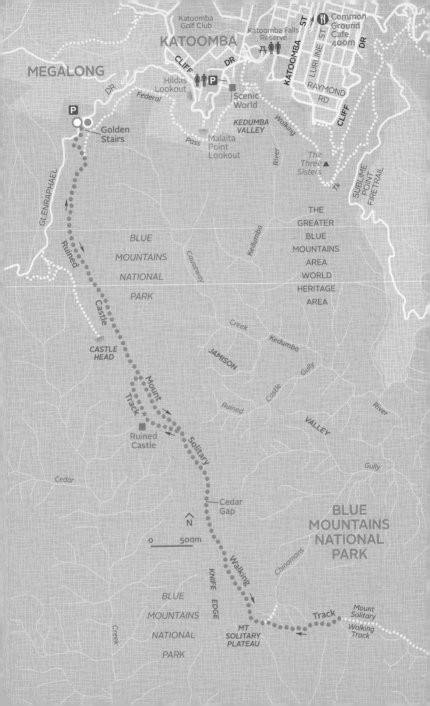

# GOLDEN STAIRS TO MT SOLITARY
## KATOOMBA

Challenging Blue Mountains walk down a cliff-face, through the heavily wooded Jamison Valley to majestic Mt Solitary.

From the Golden Stairs carpark descend the carved-sandstone steps and steel ladders 160m into the valley. Built in the 1800s, the route provided access to the Ruined Castle kerosene shale mines. At the bottom of the stairs take the track to your right and enjoy walking through groves of ferns, sassafras and coachwoods. Detour to Ruined Castle (adding an hour to your walk), which has 360-degree vistas of cliffs, gum-covered valleys and Mt Solitary. Roughly 600m on from the Ruined Castle track junction, look for the remnants of miners' cottages. Drop into Cedar Gap before climbing the steep ridge to the Knife Edge and the Mt Solitary Plateau. Return the way you came. Refuel on hearty fare at Common Ground Cafe (214 Katoomba St).

**Location**
107km west from Sydney

**Distance**
14km return

**Grade**
Medium-hard

**Ideal Season**
Winter

**Map**
UBD 29 E6

**Notes**
No dogs
Track unsealed
Steep descent
via Golden
Stairs includes
1600 steps and
steel ladders

Photo: Jamison Valley, Blue Mountains
© Tourism Australia, Sue Wright

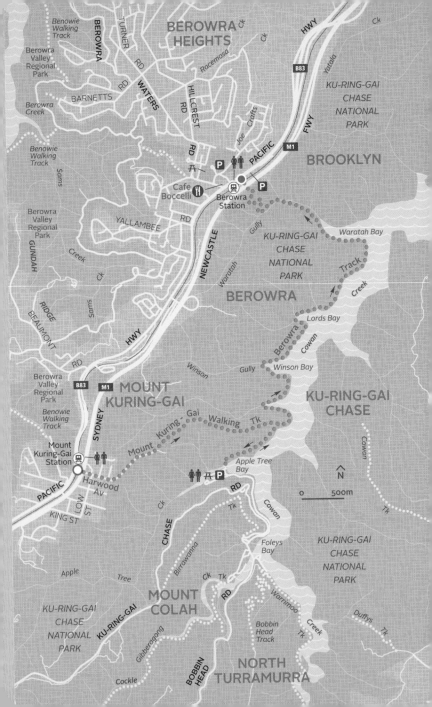

# COWAN CREEK
## MT KURING-GAI TO BEROWRA

Meandering walk along Cowan Creek taking in five enticing bays and both Indigenous and European historical sites.

From Mt Kuring-Gai Station, cross the freeway and follow Harwood Ave until it joins the narrow, sandy Mt Kuring-Gai Walking Track. Continue along the left fork and down stone steps between huge boulders to a clearing where wallabies feed at dusk. Zigzag to the foot of the hill and turn right towards Apple Tree Bay, perfect for a picnic. Return to the Mt Kuring-Gai Walking Track junction and continue north to timber boardwalks that jut over the water and a gully strewn with shell middens. Further along, just before Lords Bay, hundreds of grass trees stand to attention. At Waratah Bay inspect the remnants of an 1890s home and jetty. Walk along Waratah Gully, complete with cobblestones, uphill. At the summit cross the freeway to Berowra Station. Try the traditional Italian wood-fired pizzas at Cafe Boccelli (4 Berowra Waters Rd).

13

Location
30km north from Sydney

Distance
10.7km circuit

Grade
Medium

Ideal Season
Winter

Map
UBD 114 F11

Notes
No dogs
Track unsealed
Begins at
Mt Kuring-Gai
Station; ends at
Berowra Station

Photo: Grass trees (Xanthorrhoea)
© Amanda Slater

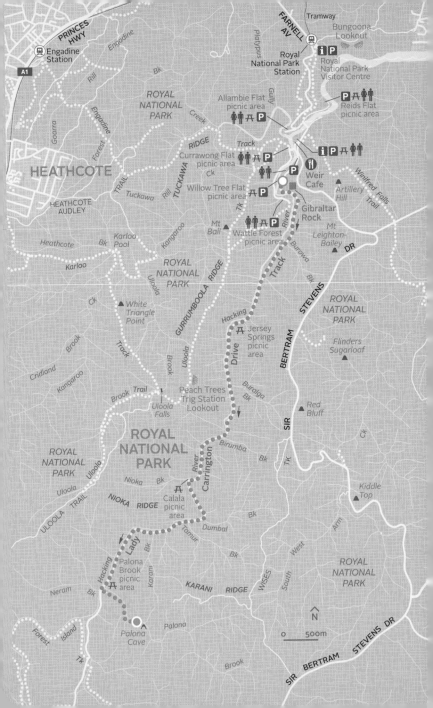

# LADY CARRINGTON
# DRIVE TO PALONA CAVE
## ROYAL NATIONAL PARK

14

Peaceful, eucalypt- and rainforest-flanked walk along a historic carriageway following the eastern bank of the Hacking River.

One of the park's early roads, Lady Carrington Dr was completed in 1886 and is now closed to vehicles. Starting at the northern end of the drive, pass through the Willow Tree Flat gate. Less than 500m along is a large overhang known as 'Gibraltar' from which the road surface was cobbled. Another 2km on is Jersey Springs – two stone troughs built in 1892 to capture water for both horses and humans (the water is no longer suitable for drinking). Calala Picnic Area, with its small sandy beach on the river, is an ideal lunch stop. Further on, take the signposted track to Palona Cave, complete with limestone columns and stalactites, and just beyond a pretty waterfall. Return to the main track and go back the way you came. Stop off at the Weir Cafe (Lady Carrington Dr) to recharge.

**Location**
37km south from Sydney

**Distance**
18km return

**Grade**
Easy-medium

**Ideal Season**
Winter

**Map**
UBD 352 J8

**Notes**
No dogs
Track unsealed
Park gates close at 8.30pm

Photo: Hacking River, Audley
© Michelle Teoh, MeltinMoments Photography

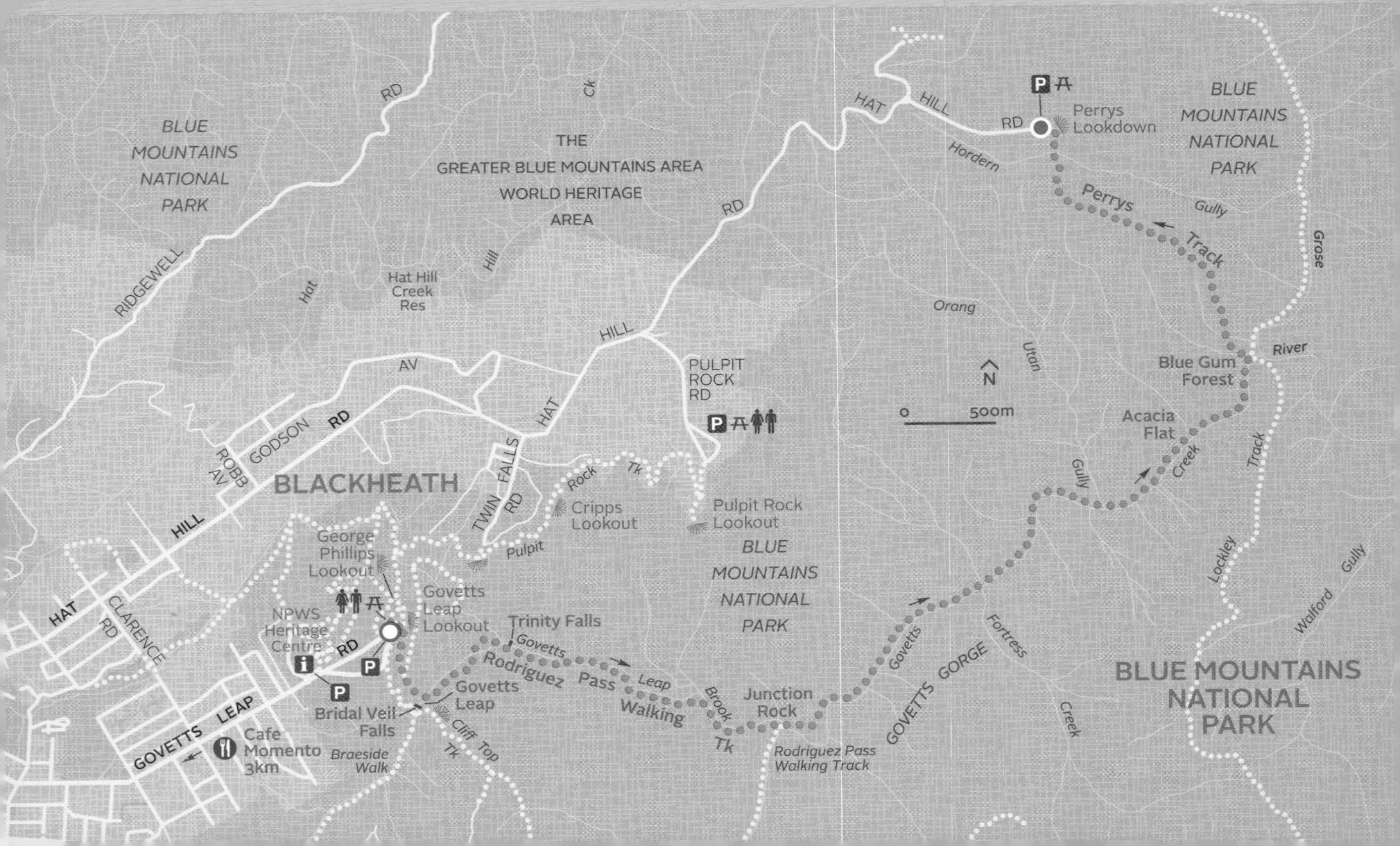
BLUE MOUNTAINS NATIONAL PARK
THE GREATER BLUE MOUNTAINS AREA WORLD HERITAGE AREA
RIDGEWELL RD
Ck
Hat
Hill
Hat Hill Creek Res
HAT HILL RD
P
Perrys Lookdown
Hordern
Perrys Track
Gully
Grose River
BLUE MOUNTAINS NATIONAL PARK
Orang
Utan
Gully
N
0 500m
Blue Gum Forest
Acacia Flat
Creek
Track
Lockley
Walford Gully
PULPIT ROCK RD
P
AV
GODSON RD
ROBB AV
BLACKHEATH
HAT HILL RD
TWIN FALLS RD
Rock Tk
Cripps Lookout
Pulpit Rock Lookout
Pulpit
BLUE MOUNTAINS NATIONAL PARK
George Phillips Lookout
Govetts Leap Lookout
NPWS Heritage Centre
RD
P
P
CLARENCE RD
Trinity Falls
Govetts Leap Brook
Rodriguez Pass Walking Tk
Junction Rock
Govetts
Fortress Creek
GOVETTS GORGE
BLUE MOUNTAINS NATIONAL PARK
Govetts Leap
Bridal Veil Falls
Cliff Top Tk
Braeside Walk
GOVETTS LEAP
Cafe Momento 3km
Rodriguez Pass Walking Track

# GOVETTS LEAP TO PERRYS LOOKDOWN
## BLACKHEATH

Magnificent Blue Mountains National Park nature walk down a sheer cliff-face and through towering Blue Gum Forest.

Starting at Govetts Leap Lookout take the signposted left-hand track down steep steps and steel ladders to the base of Bridal Veil Falls, where you'll enter a rainforest of coachwoods, birds-nest ferns, native raspberries and orchids. Cross Govetts Leap Brook twice, moving from rainforest to dry eucalypt forest. Continue along the left bank of Govetts Creek to serene Blue Gum Forest where pin-straight trees shoot 50m skyward from a carpet of green. From here you'll begin the 2.4km climb to Perrys Lookdown up stairs carved into the cliff. The final push to the summit rewards you with panoramic views. Reflect on your day's outing in the sunny patio of Cafe Momento (38 Govetts Leap Rd), which serves delicious vegetarian fare.

15

**Location**
115km west from Sydney

**Distance**
9.4km one way

**Grade**
Hard

**Ideal Season**
Winter

**Map**
UBD
Blue Mountains
7 Q6

**Notes**
No dogs
Track unsealed

Sydney

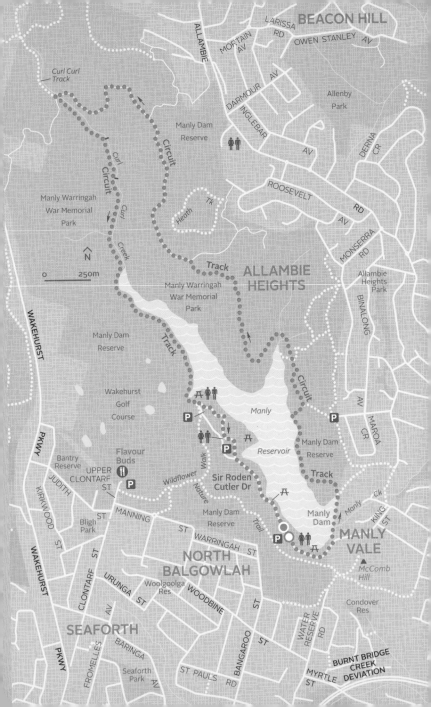

# MANLY DAM
## ALLAMBIE HEIGHTS

Secluded and spectacular lakeside circuit through wildflowers, woodland, swamp and rambling heath.

16

More than 300 native plant species have been recorded around this freshwater lake. From the King St parking area cross the dam wall and wander up the stairs enjoying the flannel flowers. Head left along the Circuit Track to the water's pebbly foreshore. Cross the footbridge and walk through stands of scribbly gum and red bloodwood before joining a sandy fire trail that crosses Curl Curl Creek. Take the path along the western bank of the creek, where trilling frogs can be heard on summer nights. From here follow the track to the junction of Wildflower Walk. Head left along the lake for a dip then continue back to the carpark. For spectacular views over the dam, try a balcony table at Flavour Buds (Upper Clontarf St).

**Location**
18km north from
Sydney

**Distance**
7.5km circuit

**Grade**
Medium

**Ideal Season**
Spring

**Map**
UBD 197 F3

**Notes**
No dogs
Track unsealed
Gates to King St
entrance open
7am-8.30pm

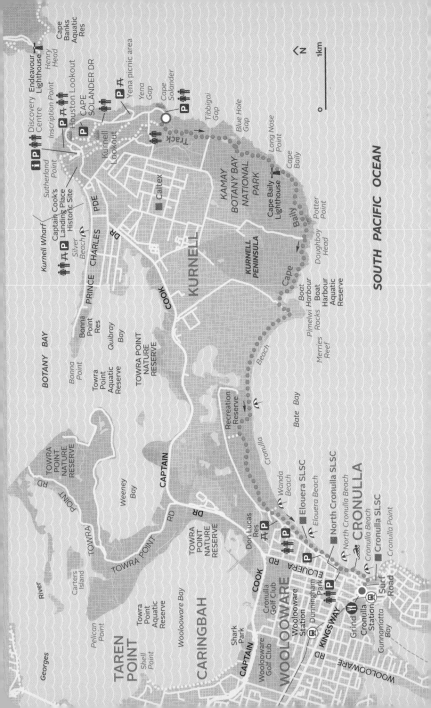

# CAPE BAILY TO CRONULLA
## KURNELL PENINSULA

17

Dramatic coastal walk along weather-ravaged cliffs, through flowering heathland and over sun-bleached sand dunes.

Starting at the end of Cape Solander Dr, trace the rock platforms at the cliff-edge south before stepping onto a sandy path through banksias filled with the chatter of honeyeaters and superb fairy wrens. Continue away from the cliff-edge, across sandstone platforms and through stunted heath until you reach a towering sand dune. Climb over it and rejoin the path as it traverses another dune and then take the short sandy sidetrack to Cape Baily Lighthouse, with its sweeping views south to Cronulla and north to the city. Back on the path, go along the cliff-top and rock platforms until they kiss the sand. Continue along the crescent of beaches, Wanda, Elouera and North Cronulla, before cooling off at Cronulla baths. Quench your thirst at Grind (6 Surf Rd), a local institution. Return the way you came.

**Location**
34km south from Sydney

**Distance**
18km return

**Grade**
Medium

**Ideal Season**
Spring

**Map**
UBD 316 N11

**Notes**
Track unsealed
No dogs
Whale-watching platform at Cape Solander

Photo: Sunrise at Cape Baily
© Ilya Genkin

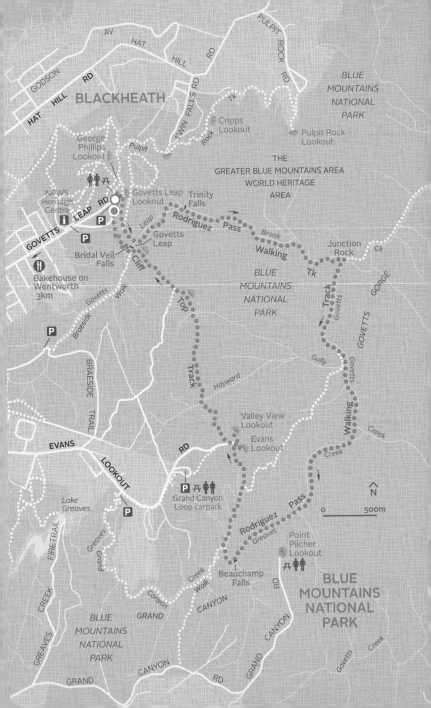

# GOVETTS LEAP
## BLACKHEATH

A heart-thumping circuit through Rodriguez Pass to Govetts Gorge, past waterfalls and towering cliffs. This walk gives you a spectacular view of the Blue Mountains.

The signposted track strikes out to the left of Govetts Leap Lookout and you'll get down the cliff using ladders and steps to the base of 180m Bridal Veil Falls. Continue along the steep track towards Junction Rock through rainforest replete with coachwoods, tree ferns and lyrebirds. From here, turn right and accompany Govetts Creek into Rodriguez Pass. Take the path that skirts Greaves Creek, pausing to admire the surrounding cliffs and bluffs. The track heads uphill to Beauchamp Falls before entering the lower reaches of the Grand Canyon. After a steep climb to Evans Lookout, regain your breath along the Cliff Top Track. Enjoy the wilderness panorama and bevy of wildflowers en route to your starting point. For the best homemade pies, try Bakehouse On Wentworth (105 Wentworth St).

**18**

**Location**
115km west from Sydney

**Distance**
11km circuit

**Grade**
Hard

**Ideal Season**
Spring

**Map**
UBD
Blue Mountains
7 P7

**Notes**
Track unsealed
No dogs

Photo: Govetts Leap
© Jennifer Morrow

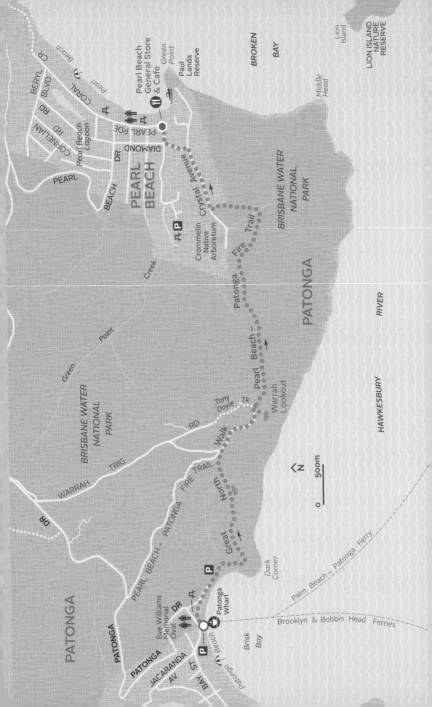

# PATONGA TO PEARL BEACH

## BRISBANE WATER NATIONAL PARK

Short but sublime coastal walk between beaches with wildflowers en masse and stunning sea vistas.

Although one of the shortest in the collection, this walk is not to be missed. It winds through native forest, offers sweeping ocean views and incorporates a wind-in-your-hair ferry ride from Palm Beach. After exiting the ferry, turn right and walk to the far end of the beach. Follow the signposted Great North Walk track uphill under a cover of sheoaks and over a tumble of granite until you reach a lookout to your right; enjoy the soothing aquamarine hues of Broken Bay from here. Keep your eyes peeled for lyrebirds, lorikeets, kookaburras and waratahs along a mostly level fire trail before beginning the gentle descent to Pearl Beach. The trail morphs into a gravel road that joins Crystal Ave. For local delights, visit the Pearl Beach General Store & Cafe (1 Pearl Pde). Return the way you came.

**Location**
100km north from Sydney

**Distance**
8km return

**Grade**
Medium

**Ideal Season**
Spring

**Map**
UBD
Central Coast
115 M12

**Notes**
Track unsealed
No dogs
Catch ferry from Palm Beach to Patonga and back

Photo: Waratahs, Warrah Trig, Brisbane Water National Park
© Doug Beckers

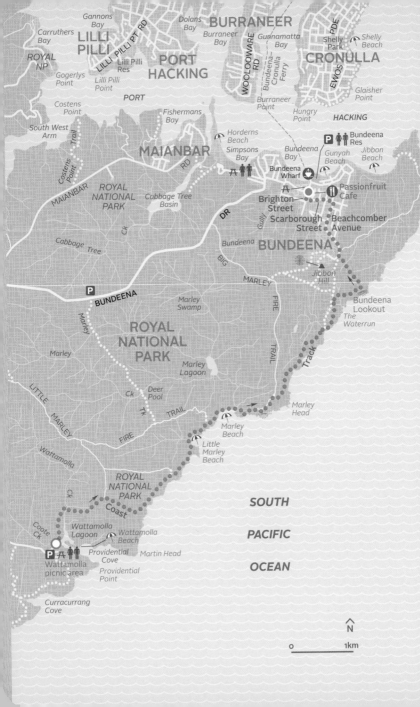

# WATTAMOLLA TO BUNDEENA
## ROYAL NATIONAL PARK

20

Stunning coastal walk with sheer sandstone cliffs, sweeping ocean vistas and Indigenous engravings.

From the carpark, head across Coote Creek and follow the Coast Track through open heath before crossing Wattamolla Creek. Head to the coast where the track runs along craggy cliff-tops and provides spectacular views. At Little Marley Beach, enjoy a dip before rejoining the track at the northern end of the sand. Next stop is Marley Beach. Its freshwater lagoon is an important wildlife refuge and was also a vital food source for the Dharawal people, whose engravings can be seen on rocks to the north. Walk along the coast enjoying flowering heathland and northerly views of the Sydney CBD. Turn into Beachcomber Ave, then into Scarborough and Brighton sts and replenish your energy reserves at the Passionfruit Cafe (Brighton St). Return the way you came.

**Location**
45km south from Sydney

**Distance**
20km return

**Grade**
Medium

**Ideal Season**
Spring

**Notes**
Track unsealed
No dogs
Avoid in hot weather

# CANBERRA
## AUSTRALIAN CAPITAL TERRITORY

From Parliament House to the mighty Murrumbidgee, the nation's capital offers a vast array of experiences for walkers. Take your lead from this well-planned and ordered city, and start at its heart, Lake Burley Griffin, before working your way out.

Follow the lakeside path as it passes instantly recognisable Canberra sites, including the Australian National War Memorial and Government House, and through beautiful gardens: in spring a riot of colour; in winter shrouded in snow and ice.

Beyond the inner-city limits, explore the eucalypt-studded hills of the suburbs, where you can join the Bicentennial National Trail, a route of over 5000km that runs from Cooktown in Queensland to Healesville in Victoria. Revel in exceptional views across rooftops to Black Mountain, the Brindabellas and beyond.

On the city's western outskirts, the Murrumbidgee flows; take your time to follow its progress as it snakes above rocky gorges and beside grassy river flats pock-marked with wombat holes and teeming with chattering cockatoos.

Finally, head into the wilds of Namadgi National Park and Tidbinbilla Nature Reserve, where you'll discover hidden rock art sites, stately stands of grass trees and the bald domes of Gibraltar Rocks, not to mention mobs of the curious characters that adorn our national coat of arms: the kangaroo and the emu.

Photo: Gibraltar Peak, Tidbinbilla © Australian Capital Tourism, Chris Holly
Photo: Grazing, part of the Poacher's Way © Australian Capital Tourism, Barb Uil

Bondo

## KEY

| | | | | | | |
|---|---|---|---|---|---|---|
| ••••• | Walk | 🎋 | Picnic area | 🍽 | Cafe/restaurant |
| ○ | Start | ☀ | Lookout | ⛴ | Ferry |
| ● | Finish | 🏖 | Beach | ® | Train station |
| → | Walk direction | 🏊 | Rock pool/baths | ⊤ | Lighthouse |
| ■ | Place of interest | P | Parking | ∧ ▲ | Cave, mountain |
| 👫 | Toilets | ℹ | Information centre | - | Waterfall |
| | | 🖐 | Indigenous culture | | |

### NEW SOUTH WALES

**21** **Kambah Pool to Casuarina Sands**
Murrumbidgee River

**22** **Yankee Hat**
Namadgi National Park

**23** **Red Hill Circuit**
Deakin–Red Hill

**24** **Cooleman Ridge**
Cooleman Ridge Nature Reserve

**25** **Watson–Mt Majura Circuit**
Hackett

**26** **Gibraltar Rocks**
Tidbinbilla Nature Reserve

**27** **West Lake**
Lake Burley Griffin

**28** **Kambah Pool to Pine Island**
Murrumbidgee River

### AUSTRALIAN CAPITAL TERRITORY

N

0     5km

**CANBERRA**

Rules Point

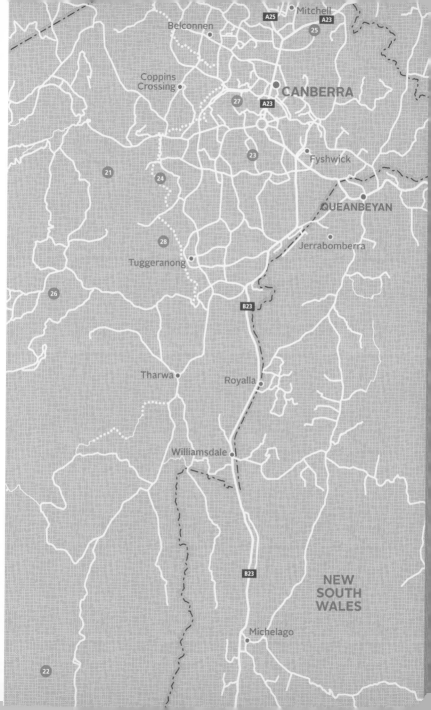

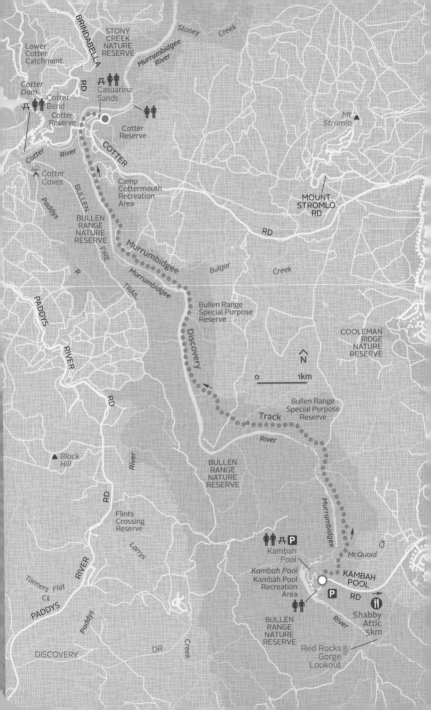

# KAMBAH POOL TO CASUARINA SANDS

## MURRUMBIDGEE RIVER

Wending trail above the Murrumbidgee River, offering mountain vistas and wildflowers in bloom, before dropping down to follow the mighty waterway.

Start at the entrance opposite the Kambah Pool carpark. Go along the single track through grassland, high above the Murrumbidgee River, before heading down a gentle slope that arcs around the nudist beach below. Take the log path to your right, cross a creek and head uphill taking in mountain vistas. Continue your uphill climb through golden wattle before heading downhill to cross a creek. Follow the path up and down, over bridges, and pass through a couple of climb-through gates. At the second, turn left keeping the fence on your right until you reach a stand of dead trees. Cross, and continue to Lunchtime Creek. Follow the path until you reach a gravel road; turn left and continue on to a track to the left with a gate. Once through it, return to the river. Veer left at the Casuarina Sands sign and climb high above the river before passing a one-lane bridge to Cotter Dam and into the carpark. On your way home, stop at Shabby Attic (3 Carleton St, Kambah) for sustenance and homewares.

**Location**
20km south-west from Canberra

**Distance**
13.8km one way

**Grade**
Medium-hard

**Ideal Season**
Summer

**Notes**
No dogs
Track unsealed
Remote region
No facilities

Photo: Casuarina Sands Reserve
© Nagappan Karuppiah

Canberra

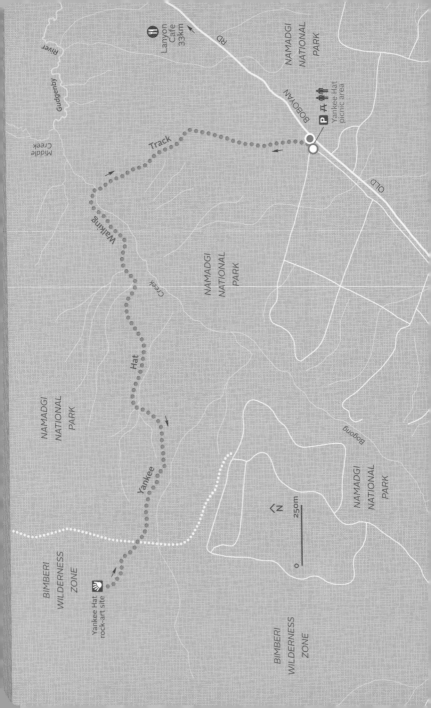

# YANKEE HAT
## NAMADGI NATIONAL PARK

Meandering track through rolling grassland to Yankee Hat Aboriginal rock-art site, with expansive mountain views and mobs of kangaroos. Named for its resemblance to the hats worn by American pioneers, Yankee Hat Mountain is your final destination in this inviting walk.

From the sign in Yankee Hat carpark, take the grass path to the right and follow the signposts through rocks down a slight slope to a lush swamp. A kilometre in, take the bridge and boardwalk across Bogong Creek, then negotiate your way around Bogong Swamp (to your left), which is dotted with delicate wildflowers. Take the path up steps to a craggy collection of rocks; there's a bench here to rest your legs. Look for eagles soaring on high. Head downhill to open grassland, over a boardwalk and towards a large, rectangular boulder nestled at the base of the mountain. Cross a bridge before heading uphill to a cluster of granite boulders complete with a shelter that houses the artwork. Don't touch; oils in your skin can damage the ochre-and-clay paint. Head back the way you came. Stop at Lanyon Cafe (15 Tharwa Dr, Tharwa), order the Grazing Plate and enjoy sublime views of the Brindabella Ranges.

**22**

Location
63km west from Canberra

Distance
6km return

Grade
Easy

Ideal Season
Summer

Notes
No dogs
Track unsealed

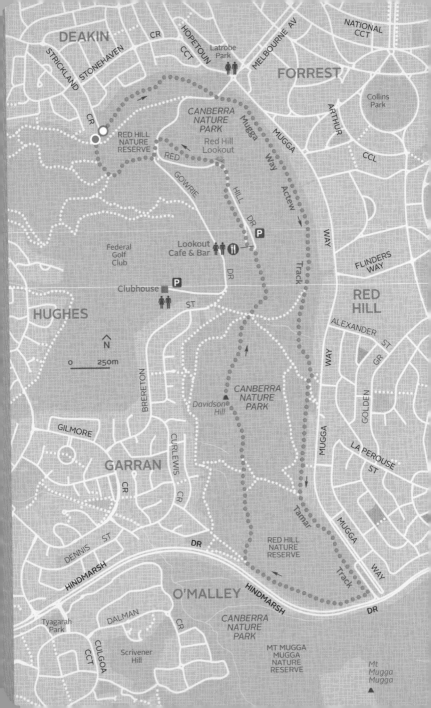

# RED HILL CIRCUIT
## DEAKIN–RED HILL

Serene woodland circuit with impressive views across central Canberra and a melodic soundtrack of native birds. Keep your dog on leash to ensure the choir doesn't flee.

Setting off from the top of Strickland Cres, climb steps up and over a dirt wall and join the Deakin Fire Trail. Follow the red-clay track through two gates (flanking Gowrie Dr) and join the Mugga Way Actew Track, listening to the chatter of crimson rosellas and the contagious laughter of kookaburras. Take the South Mugga Way Track through grassland and stands of blossoming yellow box to the Tamar Track and on to the Hindmarsh Track, with views of the Brindabellas. Pass through a gate to Davidson's Trig Track and on to the 750m peak of Davidson Hill. Head downhill before climbing to the Lookout Cafe & Bar (1 Red Hill Dr), with delicious zucchini and haloumi fritters. Go along the path to the left of the cafe to Red Hill Lookout. Near the end of the viewing area, walk through a gate and join a single dirt track that stops at a set of steps. Cross two roads, pass through a gate and onto a management road. Walk under eucalypts to a reservoir with a gate and join the fire trail that runs back to Strickland Cres.

23

**Location**
4km west from Canberra

**Distance**
9.5km circuit

**Grade**
Medium

**Ideal Season**
Autumn

**Map**
UBD 68 N5

**Notes**
Dogs permitted
Track unsealed

Photo: Expansive Central Canberra views from Red Hill Lookout
© Prescott Pym

Canberra

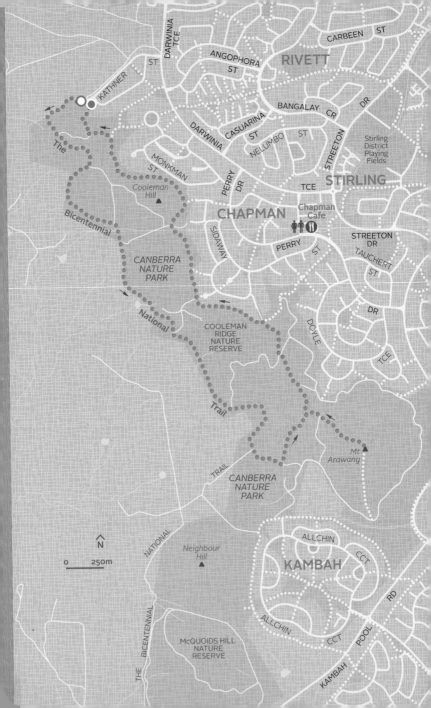

DARWINIA TCE

KATHINER ST

DARWINIA TCE

ANGOPHORA ST

CARBEEN ST

RIVETT

BANGALAY CR

STREETON DR

Stirling District Playing Fields

The

DARWINIA

CASUARINA ST

NELUMBO ST

STREETON

MONKMAN ST

PERRY DR

STIRLING

Bicentennial

Cooleman Hill ▲

CHAPMAN

TCE

Chapman Cafe

SIDAWAY

PERRY ST

STREETON DR

TAUCHERT ST

CANBERRA NATURE PARK

National

COOLEMAN RIDGE NATURE RESERVE

DOYLE

DR

TCE

Trail

Mt Arawang ▲

TRAIL

CANBERRA NATURE PARK

N̂

0   250m

NATIONAL

Neighbour Hill ▲

ALLCHIN

CCT

KAMBAH

ALLCHIN

CCT

POOL

RD

THE BICENTENNIAL

McQUOIDS HILL NATURE RESERVE

KAMBAH

# COOLEMAN RIDGE
## COOLEMAN RIDGE NATURE RESERVE

Part of the Bicentennial National Trail, a 5330km track that stretches from Queensland to Victoria, this portion passes through grassland, takes in stunning mountain vistas and includes a visit to the summit of Mt Arawang.

Park your car at the end of Kanther St and follow the equestrian track to a small dam. Cross the dam wall and continue before turning left just before a farmhouse. Climb the hill and enjoy views of the Murrumbidgee River and the Brindabellas. Skirt around a large dam, cross a creek and head uphill until the track reaches the top of the ridge where you'll see Black Mountain. Take the right-hand path towards Mt Arawang and enjoy outstanding views of Canberra. Head back the way you came; take the right fork. Follow the spine of the ridge and at the T-intersection turn left and head towards a reservoir. Keeping it to your left, go downhill through shady eucalypts to another reservoir, then go uphill until you reach a bridge and Cooleman trig point. Take the gravel road to the right and return to your starting point. At walk's end, try the lip-smacking fish and chips at Chapman Cafe (3/58 Perry Dr, Chapman).

24

**Location**
13km south-west from Canberra

**Distance**
8.5km circuit

**Grade**
Medium

**Ideal Season**
Autumn

**Map**
UBD 66 N16

**Notes**
Dogs permitted
Track unsealed

Photo: Kangaroos in the grass
© Percita Dittmar

Canberra

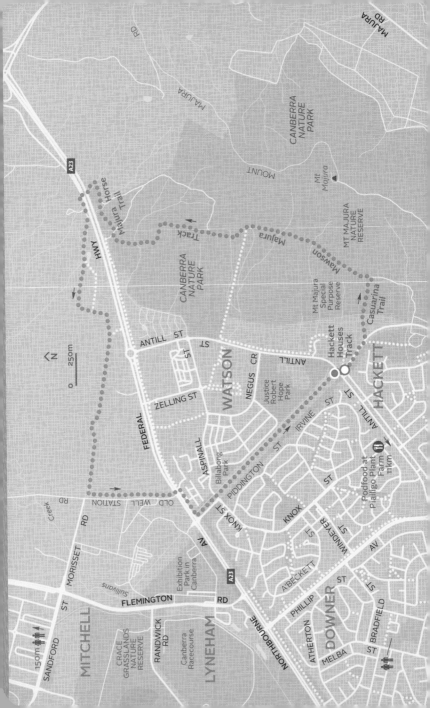

# WATSON–MT MAJURA CIRCUIT
## HACKETT

Scenic trail complete with avenues of eucalypts and spectacular views of north Canberra and Black Mountain Tower.

Fill up at Podfood at Pialligo Plant Farm (12 Beltana Rd, Canberra) before setting off from Antill St on the Hackett Houses Track. Join the Casuarina Trail and head uphill and past a dam while listening to the lively conversation of kookaburras and galahs. Take the left turn to join the Mawson Majura Track as it winds uphill. From here there are great views of the city to be had. Head through the bush to the Majura Horse Trail, which takes you to an underpass under the Federal Hwy. Once through, turn left down a gravel road and when it curves to meet the highway veer right and follow the fence-line to a paddock where you'll pick up the trail again. Turn left onto Old Well Station Rd, cross the highway and take the gravel track alongside it to a dirt path lined with towering trees on Stirling Ave. Cross Aspinall St and revel in the avenue of statuesque eucalypts that line the track back to your starting point. Look for jewel-coloured swift parrots flitting from tree to tree and hopping about in the leaf litter.

25

**Location**
9km north from Canberra

**Distance**
9km circuit

**Grade**
Medium

**Ideal Season**
Winter

**Map**
UBD 50 E1

**Notes**
Dogs permitted
Track unsealed

Photo: Swift parrot
© Alan Jordan

Canberra

RD

TIDBINBILLA

BIRRIGAI
NATURE
RESERVE

Gibraltar
Peak ▲

Gibraltar
Forest
Regeneration

Tidbinbilla

Cafe
Tidbinbilla

**i** **P**

Tidbinbilla
Visitor
Centre

TIDBINBILLA
NATURE
RESERVE

▲ Mt
Eliza

Walking

Trail

N

0 — 250m

Gibraltar

Rocks

RD

Xanthorrhoea Loop

**P**

Sheedys picnic
area

RING

TIDBINBILLA

Jedbinbilla
Special
Purpose
Reserve

**P**

Dalsetta
carpark

RD

TIDBINBILLA
NATURE
RESERVE

River

Ck

Reid

RING

Rock Valley
Homestead

Tidbinbilla

TIDBINBILLA

**P**

Flints
picnic
area

# GIBRALTAR ROCKS
## TIDBINBILLA NATURE RESERVE

Steep climb from valley, through impressive stands of grass trees *(Xanthorrhoea)* and alongside mobs of kangaroos and emus, for spectacular views atop massive granite tors.

From the Dalsetta carpark on Tidbinbilla Ring Rd take the well-signposted grass track, crossing two walkways before entering a forest of natives: banksia, wattle, apple box, grevillea and tea trees. You'll emerge into open grassland where the path climbs gently uphill. Follow the track to the Xanthorrhoea Loop, a narrow 200m path that twists through structural grass trees, before rejoining the track, now a management road. The uphill climb begins in earnest here; the road winds and rises steeply. The highest point is marked with a seat: take a rest before walking the 100m down to the rocks. Once there, take the steps up, around and between the hulking boulders until you reach a rock platform with expansive views of the valley and, faraway, Black Mountain. Return the way you came and stop at Cafe Tidbinbilla (Tidbinbilla visitor centre, Tidbinbilla Ring Rd, Paddy's River) for a hearty lunch and a locally produced coffee.

26

**Location**
45km south-west
from Canberra

**Distance**
6km return

**Grade**
Hard

**Ideal Season**
Winter

**Notes**
No dogs
Track unsealed
Exposed, steep
uphill paths

Canberra

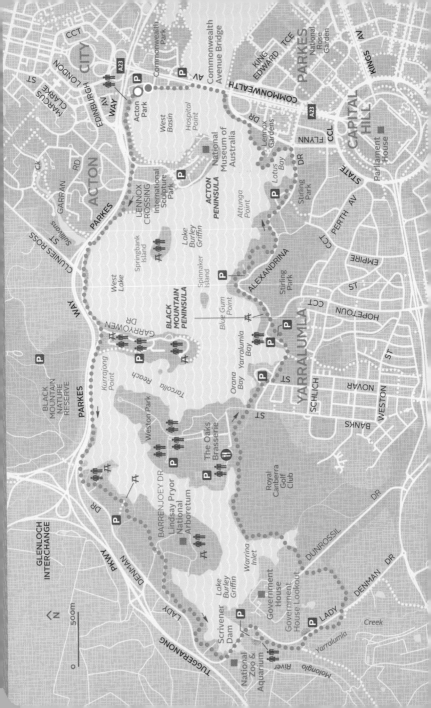

# WEST LAKE
## LAKE BURLEY GRIFFIN

Popular city path around the western banks of Lake Burley Griffin taking in iconic Canberra sites, including Government House. With so much to see you'll want to allow more than walking time to enjoy it.

Starting at Acton Park head west towards Acton Peninsula. Take the right fork and head through the underpass, over Lennox Crossing and continue down towards Sullivan's Creek bridge. The path loops to the right and under the bridge before delivering you onto its deck; cross, then take the steps down to the lakeside path and on to Black Mountain Peninsula. Cross Gary Owen Dr and go over Barrenjoey Rd to skirt the 30ha Lindsay Pryor National Arboretum. Once across Scrivener Dam, detour to Government House Lookout for views of the grand building and its 54ha of gardens and lawn. A mob of kangaroos come out of hiding around dawn and dusk. Return to the path and cross Lady Denman and Dunrossil drives into exotic Westbourne Woods. Lunch at Yarralumla Gallery and the Oaks Brasserie (1 Weston Park Rd), then continue on to Stirling Park and around into Lennox Gardens. Across the water you'll see the grand design of the National Museum. Cross Commonwealth Bridge and you're back at your starting point.

**27**

Location
Central Canberra

Distance
14.5km circuit

Grade
Easy

Map
UBD 59 F6

Ideal Season
Spring

Notes
Dogs permitted
Track sealed

Photo: Dunrossil Dr
© Teon Harasymiv

Canberra

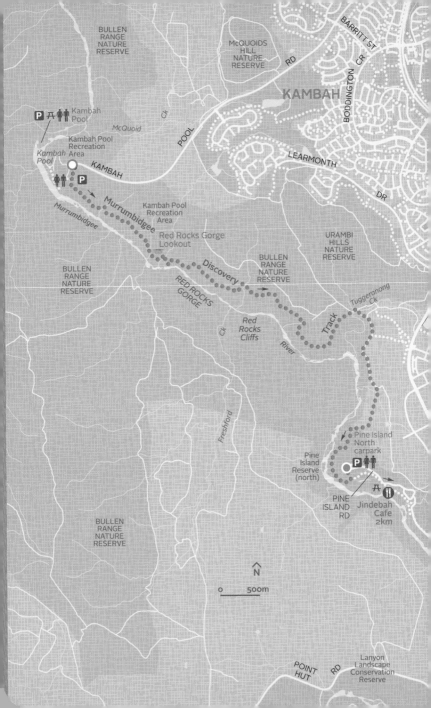

BULLEN
RANGE
NATURE
RESERVE

McQUOIDS
HILL
NATURE
RESERVE

BARRITT ST

KAMBAH

POOL RD

BODDINGTON CR

Kambah
Pool

McQuoid Ck

Kambah Pool
Recreation
Area

Kambah
Pool

KAMBAH

Murrumbidgee

Murrumbidgee

LEARMONTH

DR

Kambah Pool
Recreation
Area

Red Rocks Gorge
Lookout

Discovery

URAMBI
HILLS
NATURE
RESERVE

BULLEN
RANGE
NATURE
RESERVE

BULLEN
RANGE
NATURE
RESERVE

RED ROCKS
GORGE

Red
Rocks
Cliffs

Ck

River

Track

Tuggeranong Ck

Freshford

Pine Island
North
carpark

Pine
Island
Reserve
(north)

PINE
ISLAND RD

Jindebah
Cafe
2km

N

0    500m

BULLEN
RANGE
NATURE
RESERVE

POINT
HUT RD

Lanyon
Landscape
Conservation
Reserve

# KAMBAH POOL TO PINE ISLAND
## MURRUMBIDGEE RIVER

Elevated track following the Murrumbidgee River with blooming springtime wattle and wombats aplenty. After good rain, whitewater aficionados shoot the rapids in Red Rocks Gorge.

Enter Bullen Range Nature Reserve from the left side of Kambah Pool carpark and take the marked track to a lookout over Red Rocks Gorge. Continue on, switching from views of the river to open grassland before reaching Red Rock Cliffs. Follow the markers down a gully, through a gate, into farmland and up again. The grassy Urambi Hills are to your left. Head straight for the hills until you reach a fence. Turn right, with the fence on your left, and pass through a gate. Turn right again and take the grassed path down to Tuggeranong Creek. Rock hop across the water, turn right and follow the riverside path to the junction of the creek and the Murrumbidgee. Follow the marked track around a low, drystone wall (built by convicts), along the river and under a canopy of olive-grey wattle. Look for wombat holes. Swim here before climbing up to Pine Island North carpark via the Pine Island loop track. Jindebah Cafe (Flax House, Cowlishaw St, Tuggeranong) has award-winning, locally roasted coffee.

**Location**
20km south-west from Canberra

**Distance**
9.4km one way

**Grade**
Medium

**Ideal Season**
Spring

**Notes**
No dogs
Track unsealed
Exposed

Canberra

# MELBOURNE
## VICTORIA

The greater Melbourne region has a unique array of unspoilt natural habitats. You don't have to travel far to find yourself deep in towering eucalypt forest, exploring wetlands around historic sites, swimming in sheltered coves, or scampering along untamed cliff-tops.

At the city's heart, the Yarra River is ripe for exploration and you can follow it as it journeys through verdant parklands replete with a chorus of native birds and past impressive architecture (both historic and contemporary) to spill into Port Phillip Bay. On its eastern flank, the trail from Port Melbourne to historic St Kilda pier traces sandy beaches and is ideal for watching the playful antics of little penguins.

Head inland for walks along historic rail trails and through vineyards and farmland that feature gorgeous autumnal tones, and in spring, flowering natives bursting with colour. To the east, the Dandenong Ranges deliver cool bushland walks through majestic stands of eucalypts and ancient tree ferns that line gurgling creeks.

South of the city, the Mornington Peninsula is scribbled with trails offering a heady mix of lush gullies, monumental gums, craggy cliffs, sweeping coastline and expansive views across Port Phillip Bay and Bass Strait. The Bellarine Peninsula tempts you with its charming seaside towns, historic jetties and wild, windswept beaches.

Finally, tackle the buckled cliffs of Western Port, complete with private beaches and incredible vistas of Bass Strait.

Photo: Yarra Ranges National Park © Tourism Victoria, Richard I'Anson
Photo: Coffee from Von Haus in Crossley Street © Tourism Victoria, Mark Chew

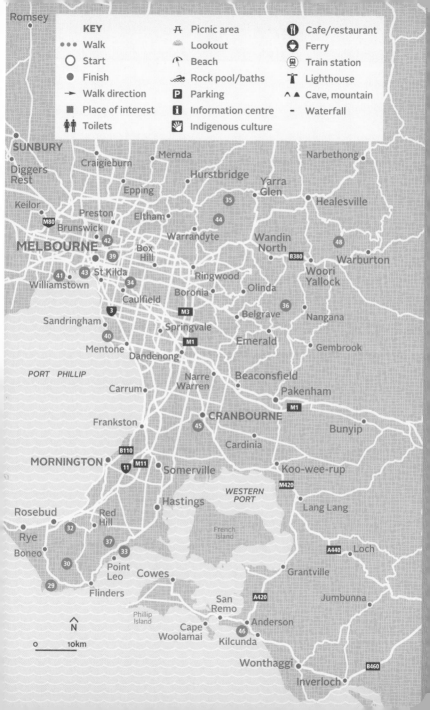

**KEY**

- ●●● Walk
- ◯ Start
- ● Finish
- → Walk direction
- ▦ Place of interest
- 🚻 Toilets
- ⅄ Picnic area
- ⚜ Lookout
- ⛱ Beach
- 🏊 Rock pool/baths
- P Parking
- ℹ Information centre
- ✋ Indigenous culture
- 🍽 Cafe/restaurant
- ⚓ Ferry
- Ⓡ Train station
- ⊤ Lighthouse
- ⋀ ▲ Cave, mountain
- − Waterfall

Romsey

SUNBURY

Diggers Rest

Keilor

Craigieburn

Mernda

Hurstbridge

Narbethong

Epping

Yarra Glen

Healesville

M80

Preston

Brunswick

Eltham

Warrandyte

35

44

Wandin North

48

MELBOURNE

42

39

Box Hill

B380

Woori Yallock

Warburton

41

43

St Kilda

Ringwood

Williamstown

34

Boronia

Olinda

Caulfield

3

Sandringham

M3

Belgrave

36

Nangana

40

Springvale

Emerald

Gembrook

Mentone

M1

Dandenong

PORT PHILLIP

Carrum

Narre Warren

Beaconsfield

Pakenham

Frankston

CRANBOURNE

M1

45

Bunyip

Cardinia

MORNINGTON

B110

11 M11

Somerville

Koo-wee-rup

Hastings

WESTERN PORT

M420

Lang Lang

Rosebud

Red Hill

French Island

32

Rye

37

Boneo

33

Grantville

30

Point Leo

Cowes

Loch

A440

29

Flinders

Phillip Island

San Remo

A420

Anderson

Jumbunna

Cape Woolamai

46

Kilcunda

N

0    10km

Wonthaggi

B460

Inverloch

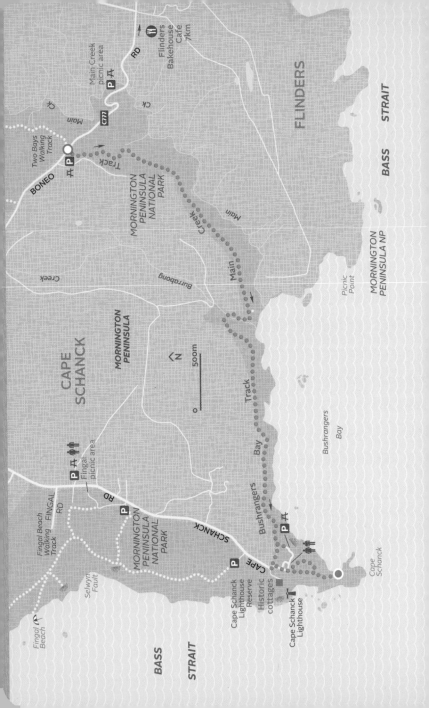

# CAPE SCHANCK
## MORNINGTON PENINSULA

A cliff-top walk from Bushrangers Bay
to Cape Schanck with eucalypts, banksias and
geological formations.

29

This is a spectacular trail, skirting rugged coastline
battered by the wild waters of Bass Strait.
Follow the Main Creek Track from the carpark to
Bushrangers Bay. The eucalypt forest gradually
gives way to shady thickets of coast banksia as
the trail comes to an isolated sandy beach fringed
by pitted basalt cliffs. Continue along the deep red
and grey cliffs to Cape Schanck. The 1850s stone
lighthouse overlooks a boardwalk that descends
the rocky promontory, which looks back over the
trail to a pebbled beach surrounded by sculptural
volcanic forms. You can find a sheltered spot
behind the lighthouse cottage for a picnic. After
returning, head to Flinders Bakehouse Cafe
(60 Cook St) for their coffee and fruit loaf.

**Location**
109km south from
Melbourne

**Distance**
13km return

**Grade**
Medium

**Ideal Season**
Summer

**Map**
Melway 259 K8
UBD 513 A7

**Notes**
Do not walk on
fire ban day
No dogs
Track unsealed

Photo: Cape Schanck
© Kasia Pawlikowski

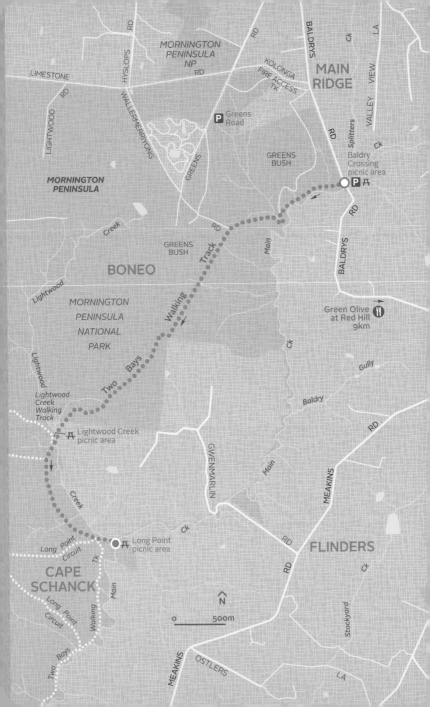

# GREENS BUSH
## MORNINGTON PENINSULA

Native bushland walk through the fern gullies and towering eucalypt forests of Mornington Peninsula National Park.

The sheltered walk follows a rippling creek through cool forest – the largest area of remnant bushland on the peninsula, and home to the largest population of eastern grey kangaroos. From the picnic area at Baldry Crossing, cross the road and take the left-most opening to the circuit track. Kangaroos, wallabies, parrots, honey eaters and black cockatoos can be seen in the bracken understorey and amongst the eucalypts. Turn left onto the Two Bays Walking Track and follow the signs toward Bushrangers Bay. Before returning, there's a restful spot for a picnic at Long Point. Visit the historic town of Flinders after the walk. After returning, head to Green Olive at Red Hill (1180 Mornington–Flinders Rd, Red Hill), for great coffee and food.

**30**

Location
103km south from
Melbourne

Distance
14km return

Grade
Medium

Ideal Season
Summer

Map
Melway 254 G6
UBD 507 M3

Notes
Do not walk on
fire ban day
No dogs
Track unsealed

Melbourne

Photo: Mornington Peninsula National Park
© Helen Grodski

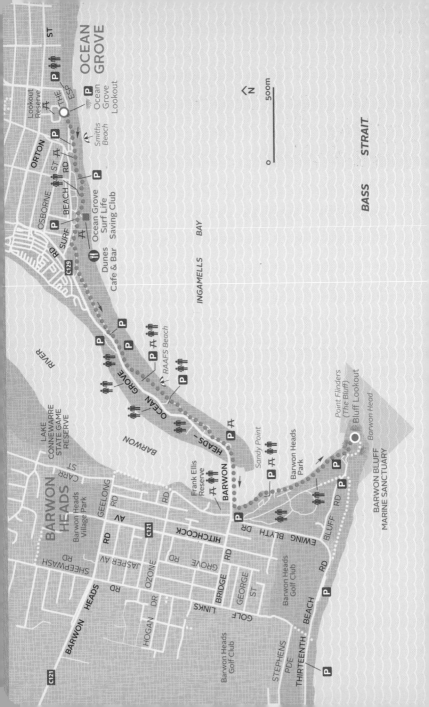

# OCEAN GROVE FORESHORE
## BELLARINE PENINSULA

31

Coastal walk from Ocean Grove to Barwon Heads along sandy beaches with native wildlife.

The seaside towns of Barwon Heads and Ocean Grove are neighbours across the Barwon River. With old jetties and timber structures, they have a charming, sleepy atmosphere. From the Lookout Reserve carpark, follow the foreshore towards Barwon Heads. Popular with surfers, the long, sandy beach undulates with fragile dunes. You will pass the Ocean Grove Surf Life Saving Club where Dunes Cafe is located (Surf Beach Rd). Have a coffee and admire the great views over the ocean. Continue on to Barwon Heads, cross the bridge over the Barwon River and walk towards the Bluff. From here, the view looks out across the beach and sweeping coastal vegetation to the Great Ocean Rd and the expansive Bass Strait. Return along the shallow Barwon River estuary, where there are lovely spots for a picnic.

**Location**
100km south-west from Melbourne

**Distance**
12km return

**Grade**
Medium

**Ideal Season**
Summer

**Map**
Melway 497 J1
UBD 664 B20

**Notes**
No dogs
Track unsealed

Melbourne

Photo: Barwon River mouth, Barwon Heads
© Tourism Victoria, Mark Chew

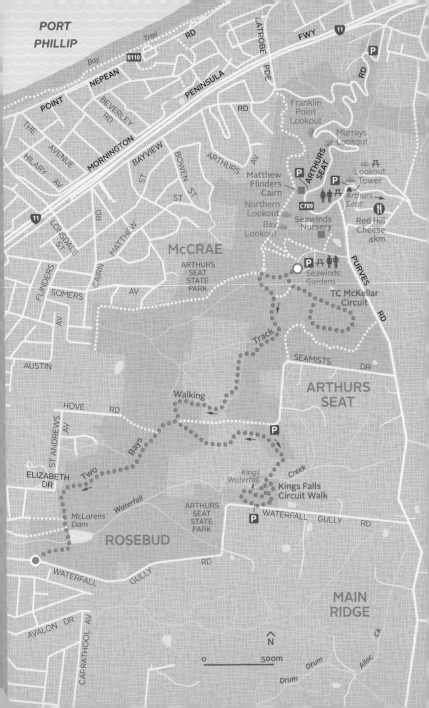

# ARTHURS SEAT
## MORNINGTON PENINSULA

A walk through eucalypt and fern forest with numerous vantage points to enjoy the expansive view of Port Phillip.

After picking up a delicious picnic lunch from Red Hill Caterers Cafe and Store (5 Mornington–Flinders Rd), head to the formal Seawinds Gardens. Lined with mature oaks, the gardens tilt toward a view of the bay and, on a clear day, you can see Melbourne's skyline, Bellarine Peninsula and the granite You Yangs. From the McKellar Circuit, turn left onto the Two Bays Walking Track. The track passes through a cross section of the peninsula's landscape: mixed eucalypt and grass tree forest gives way to ferns, including the delicate scrambling coral fern. Stop for a picnic along the way. After completing the Kings Falls Circuit Walk, continue to Waterfall Gully Rd. When you have finished, you can drop into Red Hill Cheese (81 William Rd) and sample some organic cheese.

32

**Location**
94km south from Melbourne

**Distance**
14km return

**Grade**
Medium

**Ideal Season**
Summer

**Map**
Melway 159 E12
UBD 487 H15

**Notes**
Do not walk on fire ban day
No dogs
Track unsealed

Photo: View of the bay from Seawinds Gardens
© Kevin Yank

# POINT LEO TO BALNARRING
## MORNINGTON PENINSULA

33

Coastal walk with seabirds and views across Western Port to Phillip Island and the Bass Strait.

After a picnic on the foreshore reserve, start the walk at the Point Leo Boat Club. Head toward Merricks Beach, crossing a shallow creek and passing a number of tidal rock pools. The reserve continues for the entire walk, so the beach is fringed by coastal bushland and there's plenty of bird life. Continue to Balnarring Beach, crossing Merricks Creek at the first footbridge to the Coolart Wetlands with paperbark swamps, lagoons, manicured gardens and a grand late-Victorian homestead. The area is home to swamp wallabies and many frog species. After returning the same way, head to Stonier Winery (2 Thompsons La) to relax over a cheese platter with a glass of their pinot noir or chardonnay overlooking their undulating vineyard.

**Location**
100km south from Melbourne

**Distance**
15km return

**Grade**
Easy

**Ideal Season**
Summer

**Map**
Melway 257 C6
UBD 510 D3

**Notes**
No dogs
Track unsealed

Photo: Point Leo Beach
© John Carney

Melbourne

# SOUTHBANK
## YARRA RIVER

A lively inner-city walk that crosses the Yarra, passing parklands and historic and contemporary architecture.

Meet at the Royal Botanic Gardens for an early morning picnic or have a coffee at the Observatory Cafe (Birdwood Ave). Follow the Tan Track to Boathouse Dr along the Yarra going under Princes Bridge. Continue along the Southbank and Yarra promenades past the Melbourne Convention and Exhibition Centre. Cross the river at Seafarers Bridge to Docklands passing the historic, domed Mission to Seafarers building, and walk to Victoria Harbour. Go back across Seafarers Bridge, return along the promenade and cross to Federation Square by Princes Bridge. You can have a coffee in the old brick vaults at Riverland Bar & Cafe (Vaults 1–9 Federation Wharf). Continue along the river past Birrarung Marr to the Swan St Bridge that will return you to the Botanic Gardens.

**34**

**Location**
1.3km south from Melbourne

**Distance**
10km return

**Grade**
Easy

**Ideal Season**
Autumn

**Map**
Melway 2L C2
UBD 22 L5

**Notes**
Track sealed

Photo: Royal Botanic Gardens Melbourne
© Anna Carlile

# SUGARLOAF
# RESERVOIR PARK
## CHRISTMAS HILLS

A calming walk around an expansive reservoir set in the glorious Christmas Hills abundant with wildlife.

Register with the ranger on 9844 2659 beforehand. Start with a picnic at Ridge Picnic Area – barbecues available. You can walk the entire perimeter of the reservoir, passing the Sugarloaf Sailing and Boating Club, or turn back at any point. During periods of drought, the water level can be very low. Home to eastern grey kangaroos, black-tailed wallabies, kookaburras and wedge-tailed eagles, the park has a range of vegetation types. The walk passes in and out of open dry forest, clearing to grassy shores and rolling meadows where you can sit under a tree and look out over the water. Afterwards, visit Watson's Creek Cafe & Antiques (765 Eltham–Yarra Glen Rd) for a hearty meal in the garden setting.

**Location**
52km north-east from Melbourne

**Distance**
18km circuit

**Grade**
Medium

**Ideal Season**
Autumn

**Map**
Melway 273 B2
UBD 170 J4

**Notes**
No dogs
Track unsealed

Photo: Sugarloaf Reservoir as seen from Simpson Rd
© James Caws www.jamescaws.com

Melbourne

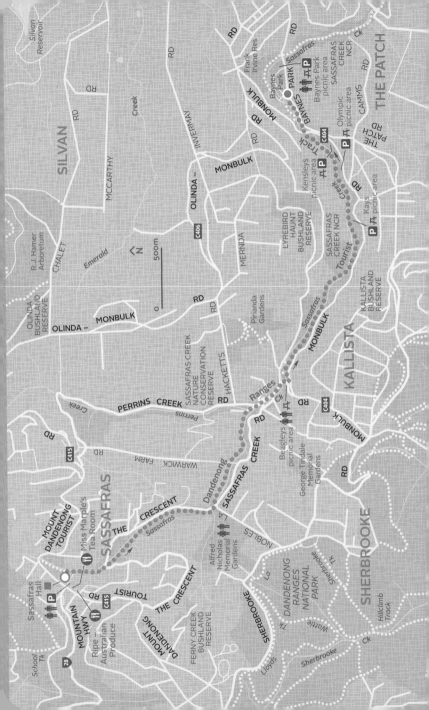

# SASSAFRAS CREEK
## DANDENONG RANGES

Cool bushland walk from Sassafras to Olinda following the eucalypts and ancient tree ferns along Sassafras Creek.

Pad the forest floor lightly to see an echidna nuzzling through leaf litter or a lyrebird skimming between the metallic mountain ash trunks and dense fern understorey. Start at Ripe – Australian Produce (376 Mt Dandenong Tourist Rd) where you can sit out on the sprawling veranda and enjoy the modern food. They also sell local produce ideal for a picnic. Beginning behind Sassafras Hall, continue along the trail following the creek. Look out for black wallabies blending into the shade. Baynes Park is a stunning wooded picnic ground. On returning, Miss Marple's Tea Room (382 Mt Dandenong Tourist Rd) serves delicious fresh scones with cream and displays unusual Agatha Christie memorabilia.

36

**Location**
43km east from Melbourne

**Distance**
15km return

**Grade**
Medium

**Ideal Season**
Autumn

**Map**
Melway 66 F9
UBD 292 A13

**Notes**
No dogs
Track unsealed

Melbourne

Photo: Fern
© Tourism Victoria, Rob Blackburn

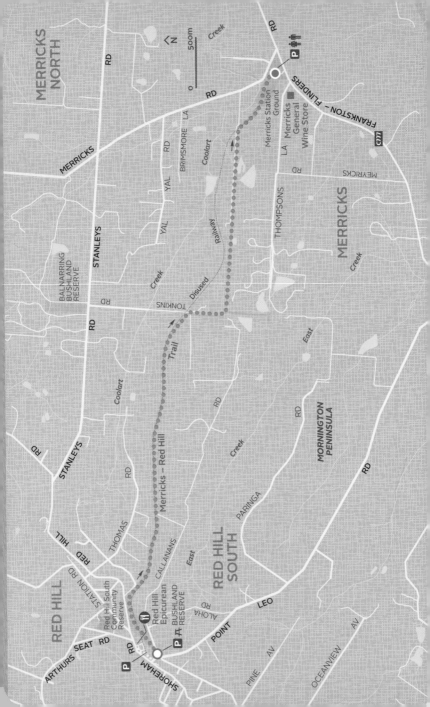

# RED HILL TO MERRICKS
## MORNINGTON PENINSULA

Leafy forest walk, past vineyards and open fields, with expansive views of the Mornington Peninsula coastline.

Head to Red Hill Epicurean (165 Shoreham Rd, Red Hill South). Backing onto the walking track near the start of the walk, this is a great spot for coffee and food. The walk starts at the Bushland Reserve carpark, Callanans Rd, and follows the Merricks–Red Hill Trail along the former apple orchard railway line. Passing old farm structures, the trail is shaded by a gentle scattering of forest that opens to a view of the hinterland, across undulating vineyards and farmland. In autumn, the vine leaves are burnt orange and the track is bathed in a warm light that makes it a perfect spot for a picnic and a glass of pinot. Take a sharp right at Tonkins Rd, continue up the hill to the viewing platform and then down to Frankston–Flinders Rd. Here you'll find Merricks General Wine Store (3460 Frankston–Flinders Rd) serving delicious gourmet food and wine.

37

**Location**
95km south from Melbourne

**Distance**
13km return

**Grade**
Medium

**Ideal Season**
Autumn

**Map**
Melway 191 A7
UBD 499 C5

**Notes**
Track unsealed

Melbourne

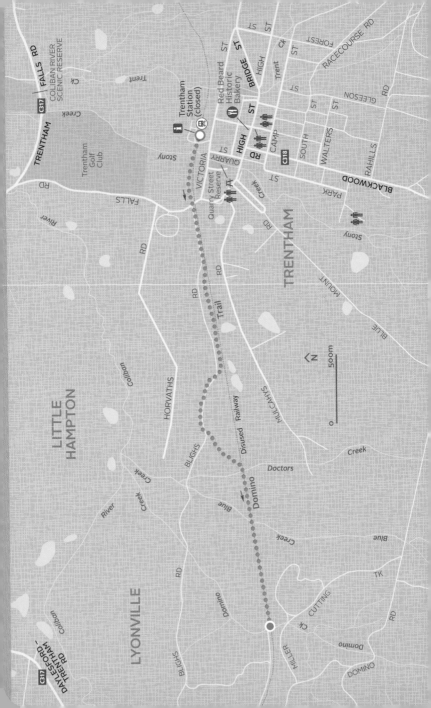

# DOMINO TRAIL
## GREAT DIVIDING RANGE

Rail trail from historic Trentham through eucalypt forest, the habitat of the endangered powerful owl.

Begin at the Red Beard Bakery (38a High St), where the 120-year-old wood-fire oven fills the rooms with the delicious smell of sourdough. The trail, beginning at the heritage-listed former railway station on Victoria St, follows the old tracks. The dense eucalypt forest, scattered with gold-rush era equipment, is invigorating in the early morning when the mist is still rising. The trail leaves the railway track at one point, passing through corridors of luscious bracken. The vegetation is kept green by underground springs. Rejoining the railway, continue until you come to the high embankment just before Domino Creek. Return to explore the well-preserved rural township of Trentham. You can have a picnic by the lake in the company of ducks.

38

**Location**
92km north-west
from Melbourne

**Distance**
10km return

**Grade**
Medium

**Ideal Season**
Autumn

**Notes**
No dogs
Track unsealed

Photo: Trentham Station
© Lynne Anderson

Melbourne

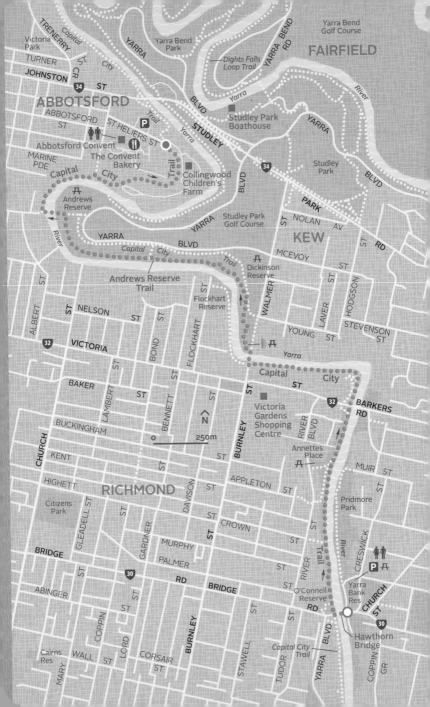

# HAWTHORN TO ABBOTSFORD
## YARRA RIVER

An undulating inner-city walk rich with birdlife following the river through Hawthorn, Richmond, and Abbotsford.

In the late afternoon, the river red gums, twisting across the narrow path, are home to bellbirds, rainbow lorikeets and kookaburras. Starting at Yarra Bank Reserve, cross the Hawthorn Bridge and follow the path along the river, crossing the footbridge onto the Capital City Trail. The trail explores some of the best-preserved native forest of inner Melbourne and is home to many native birds. Cormorants stand motionless on branches over the Yarra, airing their wings. Before the playground equipment, turn left and cross the footbridge. Descending the stairs, follow the path to the Collingwood Children's Farm and the Abbotsford Convent. The Convent Bakery (1–3 St Heliers St) serves a quinoa and pistachio porridge that's delicious, any time of day, with their Fairtrade coffee, roasted on site.

39

**Location**
5km north-east from Melbourne

**Distance**
9km return

**Grade**
Easy

**Ideal Season**
Winter

**Map**
Melway 44 K9
UBD 20 B11

**Notes**
Track sealed and unsealed

Photo: Abbotsford Convent and Collingwood Children's Farm
© Anna Carlile

Melbourne

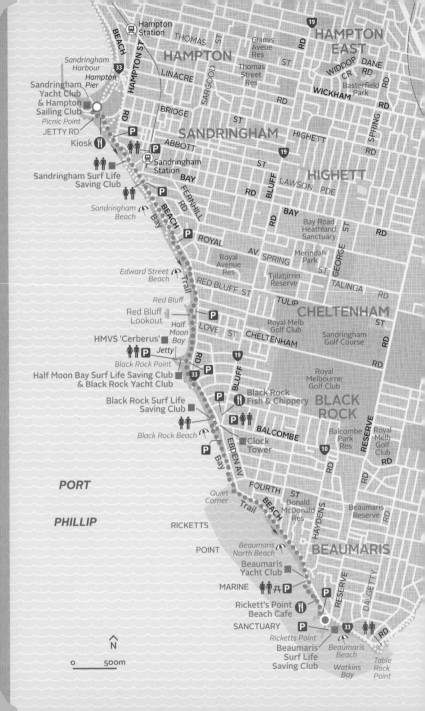

# SANDRINGHAM TO BLACK ROCK
## PORT PHILLIP

**40**

A gentle, picturesque coastal walk, passing rock pools and tea trees, with views of the bay.

Start with coffee at the kiosk at the end of Jetty Rd and then follow the long sandy coastline to Red Bluff, Half Moon Bay and Beaumaris. Black Rock Fish & Chippery (27 Bluff Rd) serves excellent crispy fish and chips. The path weaves in and out of the coastal vegetation trails before returning to the beach. This stretch is part of the Coastal Art Trail celebrating the works of Heidelberg artists including Arthur Streeton and Tom Roberts. Further on, the Ricketts Point Marine Sanctuary is a great place to explore coastal marine life. Worn sandstone cliffs fold down to the water's edge becoming easily accessible platforms and rock pools at their base.

**Location**
12km south from Melbourne

**Distance**
16km return

**Grade**
Medium

**Ideal Season**
Winter

**Map**
Melway 76 F8
UBD 344 E12

**Notes**
Track sealed

Photo: Ricketts Point Marine Sanctuary
© Lucy Pawlikowski

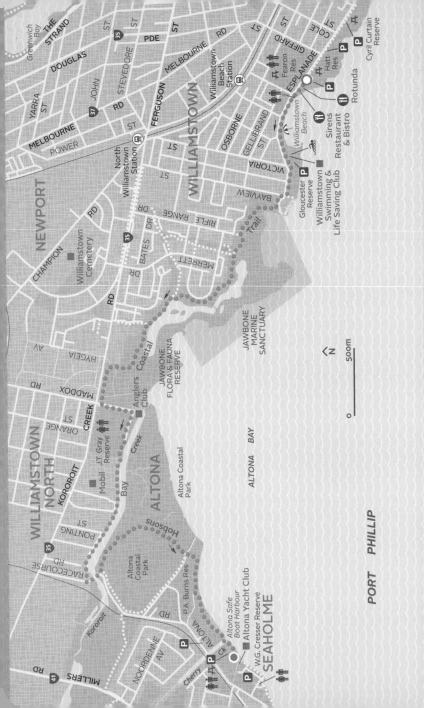

# KOROROIT CREEK
## WILLIAMSTOWN TO ALTONA

Coastal walk from Williamstown to Altona passing sandy beaches, bushlands, mangroves and wetlands.

Williamstown retains much of the architecture from its rapid gold-rush era expansion. Along the meandering coastline, this palpable history meets a natural habitat of black swans, egrets and majestic pelicans. Enjoy a coffee at the converted Rotunda cafe (The Esplanade), and follow the foreshore trail to Kororoit Creek Rd. Turn left at Maddox Rd and right at the weatherboard Anglers Club into Altona Coastal Park. Cross the creek at Racecourse Rd and continue to the Altona foreshore where you'll find plenty of cosy spots for a picnic. On returning, you can enjoy a delicious meal in the Mediterranean atmosphere of Sirens Restaurant & Bistro (The Esplanade) while enjoying the late afternoon view across the bay.

41

**Location**
14km south-west
from Melbourne

**Distance**
16km return

**Grade**
Medium

**Ideal Season**
Winter

**Map**
Melway 56 B11
UBD 281 Q18

**Notes**
Track sealed

Photo: Pelican
© Tourism Victoria, Mark Watson

# MERRI CREEK
## CLIFTON HILL

Inner-city walk following a creek through unfolding layers of Melbourne's diverse history.

Waterways say a great deal about a city. After heavy native-plant rejuvenation in recent years, this is now a pleasantly characterful trail. From Dights Falls, the walk starts out along a wide gushing creek. The path crisscrosses the creek and goes under several road bridges dating from vastly different eras. At times the area feels like a wildly overgrown London park. There are sheltered picnic areas along the trail. Cross the steel bridge at Rushall Station and follow the signs straight and then left to rejoin the river. Cross the bridge at St Georges Rd and continue to CERES, an environmental park and farm with an organic market every Saturday. The CERES Cafe (8 Lee St) serves organic food and bustles with activity over the weekend – fortunately there's plenty of seating.

42

Location
8km north-east
from Melbourne

Distance
14km return

Grade
Easy

Ideal Season
Winter

Map
Melway 2D F6
UBD 15 P11

Notes
Track sealed

Melbourne

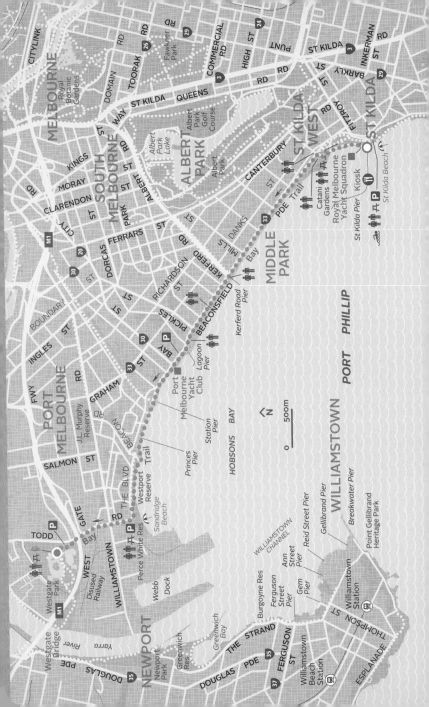

# ST KILDA TO PORT MELBOURNE
## PORT PHILLIP

A bayside walk along sandy beaches, passing old jetties and native wildlife.

Start by enjoying a coffee at the Kiosk (St Kilda Pier) surrounded by the glassy waters of Port Phillip. You may even see little penguins swimming below. The pier is an integral part of St Kilda's peculiar past, from luxury resort town to wartime playground and urban ghetto – it's now a thriving cosmopolitan community. Follow Beaconsfield Pde around in the direction of Port Melbourne. The long stretches of sandy beach, lapped by calm waves, are well attended by locals. Continue on to the Boulevard, turning right at Todd Rd to Westgate Park for a picnic. With successful native re-vegetation, the park is thriving with birdlife, including stilts and pelicans.

**43**

**Location**
7km south from Melbourne

**Distance**
14km return

**Grade**
Easy

**Ideal Season**
Winter

**Map**
Melway 2N H7
UBD 26 D12

**Notes**
Track sealed

Melbourne

# WARRANDYTE
## YARRA RIVER

Winding river walk from Stiggants Reserve to Warrandyte State Park with abundant native animal life.

Warrandyte seems far removed from urban Melbourne: here the Yarra is a little wider and, in spring, the wattles bloom with a little more radiance. From Stiggants Reserve, follow the track along the river to the Bakery (193 Yarra St), a good spot to buy a picnic lunch or continue along the river to Stonehouse Cafe Restaurant (321 Warrandyte-Ringwood Rd) for a coffee or light meal on the veranda amongst the eastern rosellas. Their gift shop has a fine array of local pottery, silk scarves and sculpted hardwood. Turn left onto Tills Dr and follow the road until the path veers right into Warrandyte State Park. The teeming ecology of kangaroos, wallabies, platypus, creeper orchids and silver wattles makes it a favourite stomping ground for bush walkers. At Jumping Creek, there is a beautiful picnic area where you could stop for lunch. Follow the river up to Blue Tongue Bend, then return on the same path.

44

**Location**
30km north-east from Melbourne

**Distance**
15km return

**Grade**
Medium

**Ideal Season**
Spring

**Map**
Melway 23 D12
UBD 198 N20

**Notes**
No dogs
Track sealed and unsealed

Photo: Blue Tongue Bend, Jumping Creek
© Alpha Lau flickr.com/avlxyz

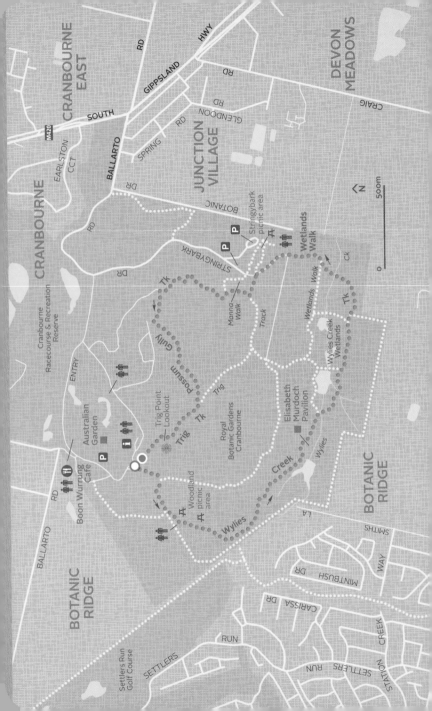

# ROYAL BOTANIC GARDENS
## CRANBOURNE

45

Colourful native bushland walk through the gardens past dense grasses, wildflowers and eucalypts.

Explore the pristine wetlands, heaths, and woodlands of the Royal Botanic Gardens, Cranbourne. Start with the Australian Garden (entrance fee) to miss the crowd and then follow trails around the parklands. The array of native flowering plants, including brilliant orange banksias and native jasmine, are a must view; in spring, there's a vibrant covering of wildflowers. Arrive early to see the sand garden against the grey foliage and prehistoric cycads in the morning light. The Boon Wurrung Cafe, designed by Melbourne architect Kerstin Thompson, melds sensitively with the landscape and serves modern food using native ingredients – the paperbark-smoked salmon is as delicious as it sounds. The rest of the gardens offer a rich mixture of vegetation types.

**Location**
53km south-east from Melbourne

**Distance**
9km return

**Grade**
Medium

**Ideal Season**
Spring

**Map**
Melway 133 G10
UBD 430 E11

**Notes**
No dogs
Track sealed and unsealed

Photo: The Australian Garden, Royal Botanic Gardens
© Anna Carlile

Melbourne

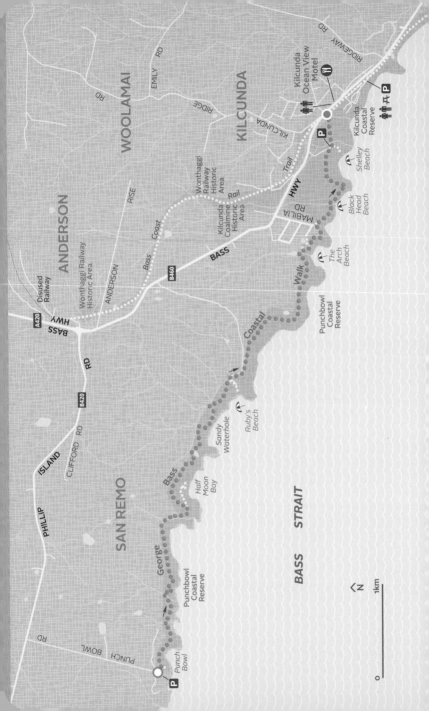

# SAN REMO TO KILCUNDA
## WESTERN PORT

**46**

Cliff-top walk with expansive views of the turbulent Bass Strait, dipping down to secluded beaches.

The George Bass Coastal Walk follows a track along enormous cliffs buckled into dramatic forms. Starting at the southern end of Punch Bowl Rd, follow the fence line along the cliff-top, toward Kilcunda. You can go down the steps to Half Moon Bay, a beach made private by weathered rocky outcrops and coast banksia, for a picnic. These beaches are too dangerous for swimming, and you need to be careful of high tides. Return up the steps and continue along the cliff-top track. From here the trail again follows the grassy cliffs and the fence line before coming to Mabilla St and then Shelley Beach. Kilcunda Ocean View Motel (3529 Bass Hwy) is a spectacular spot to have a light seafood lunch. Return the same way you came.

**Location**
122km south-east from Melbourne

**Distance**
15km return

**Grade**
Medium

**Ideal Season**
Spring

**Notes**
No dogs
Track sealed

Melbourne

Photo: George Bass Coastal Walk
© flickr.com/photos/xlynx

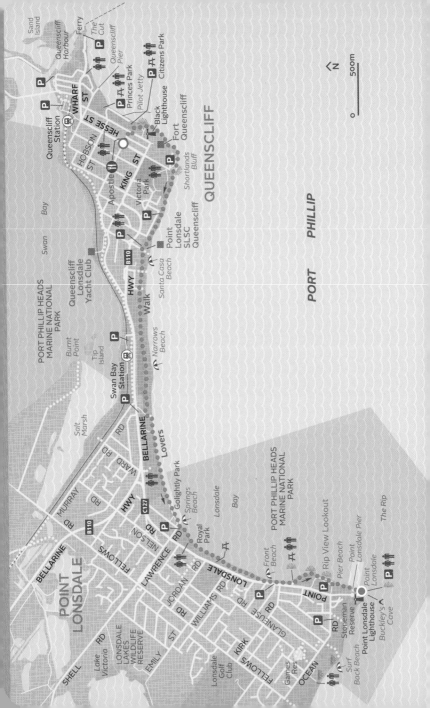

# QUEENSCLIFF TO POINT LONSDALE
## BELLARINE PENINSULA

Coastal walk between two historic lighthouses with views of Port Phillip shipping channel.

After a coffee at the Apostle (79 Hesse St), an old church complete with candelabra, start at the stone 1860s Queenscliff Lighthouse. Follow the foreshore trail along the sandy beaches toward Point Lonsdale. Rip View Lookout has incredible views out across the Rip to Point Nepean. Due to rips, this section of beach is unsafe for swimming. Continue on to the Point Lonsdale Lighthouse and Buckleys Cave. Low tide exposes impressive rock formations along this stretch. Around the point you'll come to Surf Back Beach, a wide sandy beach overlooking Bass Strait, which is perfect (and safe) for swimming. You can enjoy a picnic here before returning the same way.

**Location**
105km south-west from Melbourne

**Distance**
14km return

**Grade**
Medium

**Ideal Season**
Spring

**Map**
Melway 500 K1
UBD 667 A19

**Notes**
No dogs
Track sealed
and unsealed

Melbourne

# O'SHANNASSY
# AQUEDUCT TRAIL
## YARRA RANGES NATIONAL PARK

A cool, moist forest walk through ferns, towering eucalypts, with views of the Upper Yarra Valley.

The trail follows a decommissioned aqueduct through thick layers of forest, protected for water catchment for over a century. Entering the trail at Yuonga Rd, you are soon in the middle of dense vegetation. Mountain ash trunks lunge upward scattering light over a tapestry of rough tree ferns. Home to eastern rosellas and yellow-tailed black cockatoos, the forest opens to patches of grasslands, creeks and small waterfalls. You can continue to Dee River or return at any point. Afterwards, enjoy a picnic along the river in the township of Warburton. In the late afternoon, the lavender and chai scones are delicious accompaniments to a cup of specialty tea at the Old Tea Shop (3393 Warburton Hwy).

48

**Location**
75km east from Melbourne

**Distance**
14km return

**Grade**
Medium

**Ideal Season**
Spring

**Map**
Melway 290 E2
UBD 209 M18

**Notes**
No dogs
Track unsealed

Photo: Yarra Ranges National Park
© Tourism Victoria, Richard I'Anson

Melbourne

# ADELAIDE
## SOUTH AUSTRALIA

For easy access to coast and range walks, Adelaide is hard to beat. Just 20 minutes from the heart of town you'll find yourself exploring the cliff-lined gorges and timbered ridges of the Mt Lofty Ranges.

On its long run northward to the Flinders Ranges, the popular 1200km Heysen Trail rambles through a rolling patchwork of parks, farmland and forest. By sampling the trail you get to wander amid the inspiration for Sir Hans Heysen, one of Australia's greatest artists and nature-lovers.

Walks here also pass through the nation's wine heartland, so you're never far from famed vineyards like those that adorn Clare, McLaren Vale and the Barossa Valley. Here walking is enriched by the essence of place: great local produce, fine vintages and strong links to history and community.

Further south, as the Fleurieu Peninsula swings to the sea, there is the chance to delve into one of SA's most dramatic coastlines. From the coves and headlands of Deep Creek to the sheer cliffs at Waitpinga, this is a captivating shoreline. It encompasses not just small craggy granite islands and the expansive views of Kangaroo Island but a taste of the Southern Ocean's grandeur – from rolling ocean swells to winter sightings of whales and soaring seabirds.

Photo: Flinders Ranges and Outback © SATC, Neale Winter
Photo: Homemade scones with olives on the table © librakv Shutterstock.com

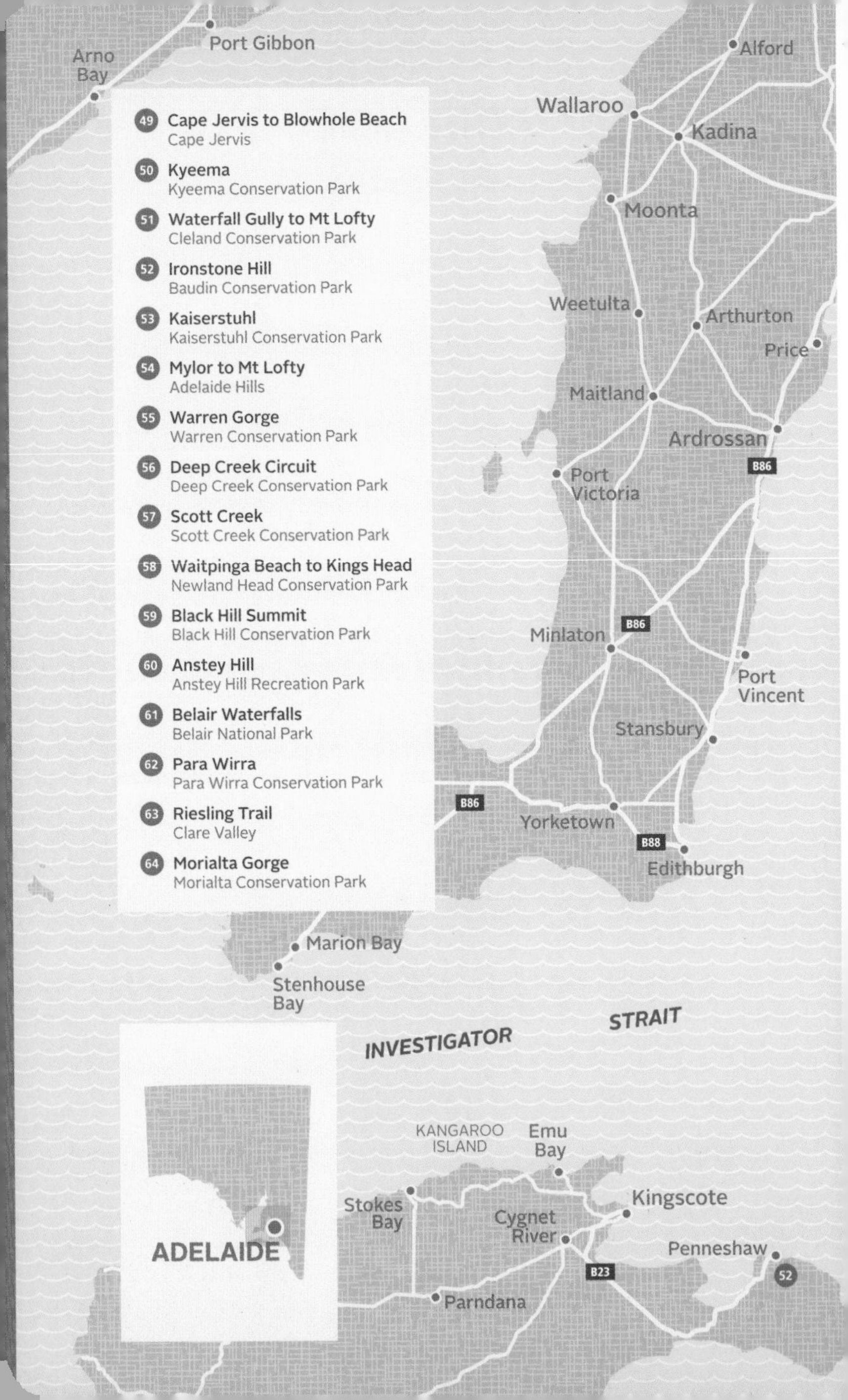

Arno Bay

Port Gibbon

Alford

Wallaroo

Kadina

Moonta

Weetulta

Arthurton

Price

Maitland

Ardrossan

B86

Port Victoria

Minlaton

B86

Port Vincent

Stansbury

B86

Yorketown

B88

Edithburgh

Marion Bay

Stenhouse Bay

INVESTIGATOR STRAIT

ADELAIDE

KANGAROO ISLAND

Emu Bay

Stokes Bay

Kingscote

Cygnet River

Penneshaw

B23

52

Parndana

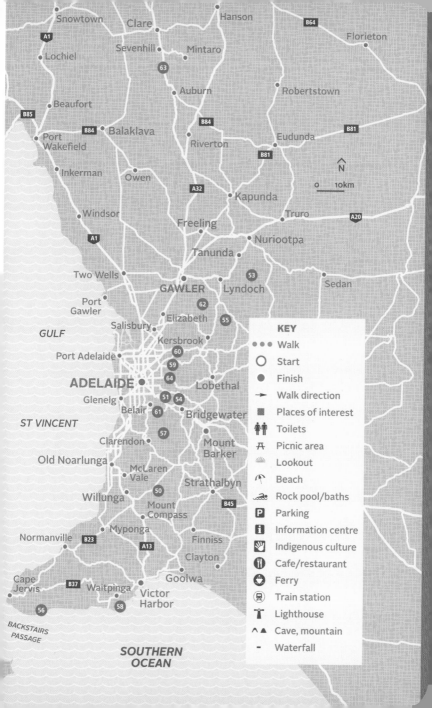

# CAPE JERVIS TO BLOWHOLE BEACH

## CAPE JERVIS

Rocky, windswept shores, island vistas and beach hideaways feature in this coastal excursion – the Heysen Trail's opening stanza.

From just above the Ferry Terminal, the trail ambles south along the low cliffs and dunes to Lands End. Beyond this knoll, the route swings slowly south-east and trends slightly inland to reach Fishery Beach – the departure point for Kangaroo Island's power cable running to Cuttlefish Bay. For the next 3km the walk grows ever-more dramatic as it leaves open grazing land and skirts the dark, rocky shores and steep gullies that dominate this rugged flank of Fleurieu Peninsula. There are also distant views across Backstairs Passage to Cape Coutts and Cape St Albans on Kangaroo Island. One final steep dip leads to the ravine of Blowhole Creek and its beach framed by craggy headlands. Finish the walk at the carpark at the end of Blowhole Creek Rd. On your way home replenish your energy stores at Jetty Food Store in Normanville (Main Rd) or Lilla's (117 Main South Rd) in Yankalilla.

**49**

**Location**
100km south-west from Adelaide

**Distance**
17km return

**Grade**
Medium

**Ideal Season**
Summer

**Notes**
Dogs permitted
Track unsealed
Exposed coastline
Blowhole Beach is four-wheel-drive access only

Photo: Blowhole Beach
© Lesley Ng

Adelaide
―――――

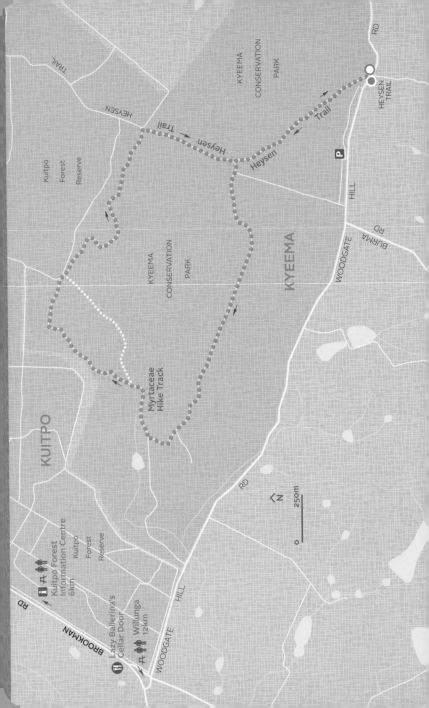

# KYEEMA

## KYEEMA CONSERVATION PARK

Gentle loop walk exploring a sheltered, mixed-eucalypt woodland in the heart of the Mt Lofty Ranges. As well as natural regeneration after a succession of major bushfires, this park also features many cleared areas that are being re-vegetated.

Follow the Heysen Trail north-west from its crossing of Woodgate Hill Rd. This opening leg crosses one of the re-vegetated patches. After around 800m leave the Heysen Trail and turn left onto a wide fire track heading west. This leads all the way to a gate on the western edge of the forest. Stay inside the park and take the Myrtaceae Hike Track heading east. After 300m, head left onto the Fire Trail and follow this onto higher ground. Arriving at the boundary, stay inside the fence to walk the narrow trail that winds back east to intersect with the Heysen Trail. Turn right and follow the Trail south back to the start. On weekends, refuel on delectable vino and wholesome pizzas at Lazy Ballerina's Cellar Door (1152 Brookman Rd).

**50**

**Location**
60km south from Adelaide

**Distance**
6km circuit

**Grade**
Easy

**Ideal Season**
Summer

**Notes**
No dogs
Track unsealed

Photo: Kyeema, Adelaide Hills
© Gary Hayes

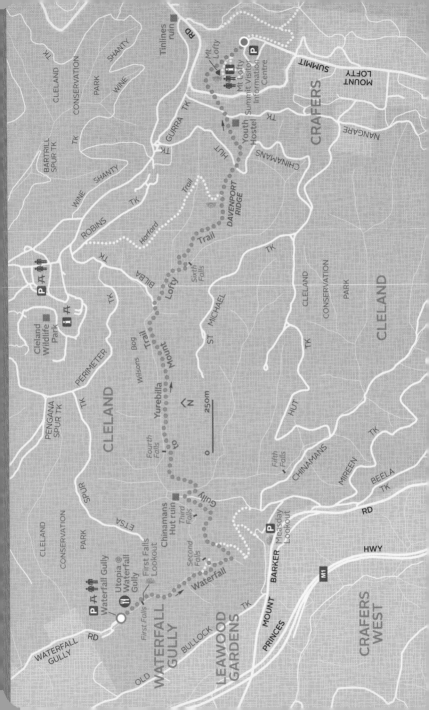

# WATERFALL GULLY TO MT LOFTY

## CLELAND CONSERVATION PARK

**51**

Ever-popular walk – and workout – ascends from the cool depths of Waterfall Gully to the thickly wooded crown of the hill's high point.

For a pre-climb coffee or sustenance, visit Utopia@Waterfall Gully (170 Waterfall Gully Rd). The walk starts from near the First Falls Lookout. About 500m on you come to the Second Falls. From there the well-made path keeps climbing steeply past the ruins of Chinamans Hut and then Wilsons Bog. Lush ferns festoon the track here, which becomes slippery after heavy rains; an array of woodland birds flourish among these damp gullies. On the way up, keep an eye out for koalas dozing in the treetops. Stay right at the junction with the Bilba Track to pass the Sixth Falls. Davenport Ridge leads upwards past the Youth Hostel and then it's a quick crossing of Mt Lofty Summit Rd before the final pinch to the top with its famous obelisk, cafe and views aplenty. Head back the way you came.

**Location**
8km east from Adelaide

**Distance**
7.5km return

**Grade**
Hard

**Ideal Season**
Summer

**Map**
UBD 132 F14

**Ideal season**
Summer

**Notes**
No dogs
Track unsealed
Steep terrain

Photo: Koala dozing in a gum tree
© Graham Watson

Adelaide
---------

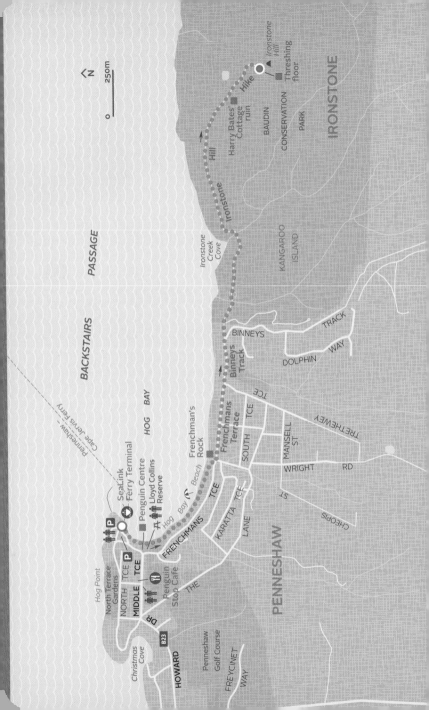

# IRONSTONE HILL
## BAUDIN CONSERVATION PARK

Seaside ramble offering dramatic outlooks from Kangaroo Island to the mainland, plus beach encounters, pioneering history and endearing wildlife.

From Penneshaw's ferry terminal, head east along the foreshore. (On Farmer's Market days, when there are half-price ferries to Penneshaw, linger in town to stock up on coffee and snacks.) Stroll the sands of Hog Bay Beach to Frenchman's Rock with its distinctive white dome commemorating the 1802 Baudin expedition. Head up to the road and take the esplanade – Frenchman's Tce, then Binneys Track – till you reach Baudin Conservation Park. The path keeps to the foreshore past Ironstone Creek Cove before climbing through whispering groves of drooping sheoak. This is an old bullock track leading to Ironstone Hill and the ruins and threshing floor of the Bates' farm that operated here from 1861. Along the way keep an eye out for Tammar wallabies and endangered glossy-black cockatoos feeding in the sheoaks. Return the way you came – and grab a tasty bite at Penneshaw's Penguin Stop Cafe (Middle Tce).

52

**Location**
114km south-west
from Adelaide

**Distance**
8km return

**Grade**
Medium

**Ideal Season**
Summer

**Notes**
No dogs
Track sealed
and unsealed
Steep terrain

Adelaide

Photo: Ironstone Hill looking across Backstairs Passage to mainland Australia
© Quentin Chester

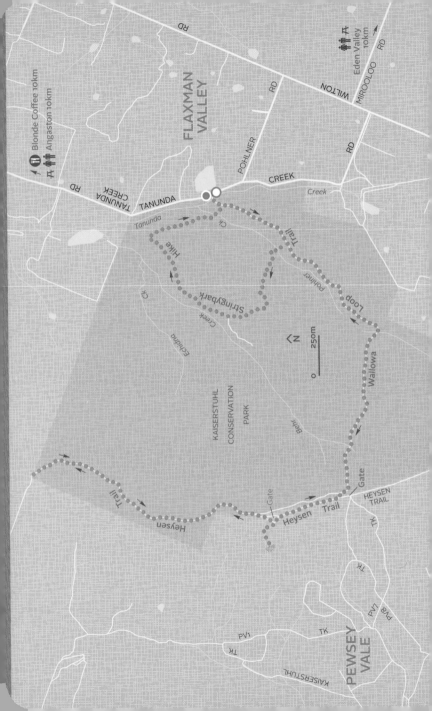

# KAISERSTUHL
## KAISERSTUHL CONSERVATION PARK

Granite tors, creeks, sheltered woodland and outstanding views of the famed Barossa Valley feature in this high country walk.

From the park's main gate on Tanunda Creek Road head left along the Wallowa Loop Trail. This track eases through low-lying banksia scrub and wetland sedges flourishing beside Pohlner Creek. Heading west the trail climbs towards the park's boundary. Turn right just before the gate and follow the Heysen Trail along the ridgeline with its granite blocks. At a second gate 500m on, a short signposted detour leads to an outcrop lookout with fine valley and distant vineyard views. Back on the main path, continue northwards for approximately another 1.5km to reach the end of the Wallowa Loop Trail (and the park's northern boundary). From here, return the way you came until you reach the Stringybark Loop Trail. Turn left onto it and follow it north and east as it swings through stringybark forests to the park's main gate. Cellar doors galore (not far away) are great for quenching the thirst; for a food recharge try Blonde Coffee (2/60 Murray St, Angaston).

**53**

**Location**
80km north-east from Adelaide

**Distance**
12km return

**Grade**
Medium

**Map**
Not in Adelaide UBD

**Ideal Season**
Autumn

**Notes**
No dogs
Track unsealed
Wildflowers in early spring

Photo: Granite tor in Kaiserstuhl Conservation Park
© Ian Riley

Adelaide

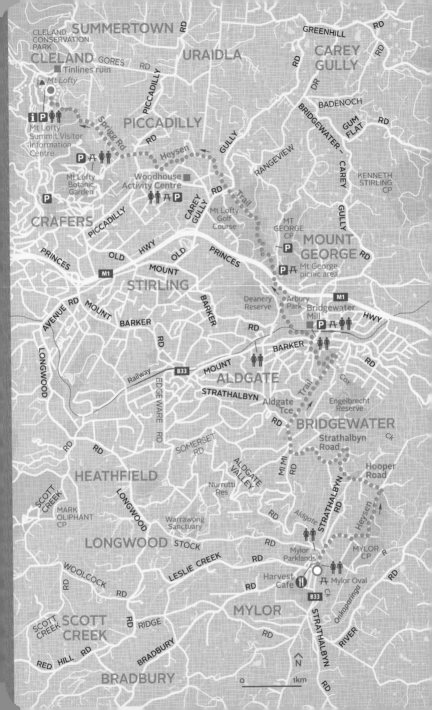

# MYLOR TO MT LOFTY
## ADELAIDE HILLS

Part of SA's iconic 1200km Heysen Trail, this classic pilgrimage winds though the hamlets and byways in the historic heart of the hills – leading all the way to Mt Lofty's atmospheric summit.

After a pre-walk bite at Harvest Cafe (240 Strathalbyn Rd) get going on the trail from Mylor's delightful main street. Just past Aldgate Creek, follow the trail eastward before it rises alongside Strathalbyn Rd. Turn right onto Aldgate Tce to drop down to Cox Creek. The winding stream-side path leads past the iconic Bridgewater Mill and onwards to Deanery Reserve and Arbury Park. A handy tunnel takes you under the freeway and through the tall timber at the foot of Mt George. A few steepish ridges lead to easier going through the Mt Lofty Golf Course and Woodhouse. From here the trail dips into Piccadilly Valley before a final push up Sprigg Rd to the steep stringybark forest. Atop the mount take a breather and enjoy one of the best city vistas in the land – there's a cafe on site too.

54

**Location**
100km south-west from Adelaide

**Distance**
17km return

**Grade**
Medium

**Ideal Season**
Autumn

**Map**
UBD 158 F14

**Notes**
Dogs permitted
Track sealed
and unsealed
Steep terrain

Photo: View from Mt Lofty summit
© Gang Chen

Adelaide
―――――
123

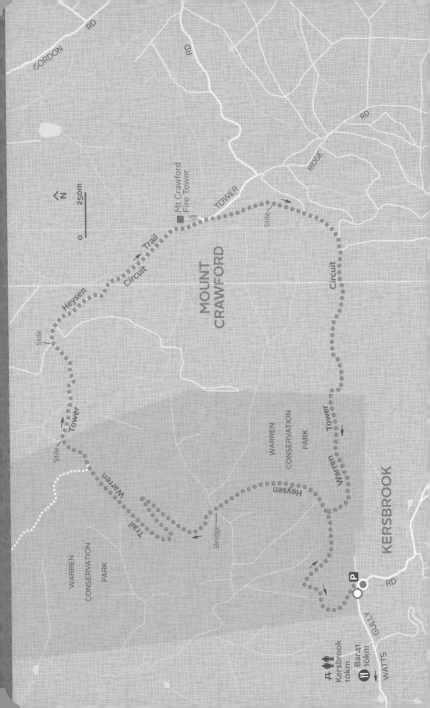

# WARREN GORGE
## WARREN CONSERVATION PARK

Challenging walk tackling robust terrain through diverse plant communities in the northern reaches of the Mt Lofty Ranges.

The walk kicks off from the park entrance on Watts Gully Rd with a gentle 1km stroll through grassy open woodland. Turn left to continue along the Heysen Trail as it contours down into Warren Gorge. Beyond a footbridge, the trail starts to travel uphill. At the saddle on the ridge-crest, continue on the Heysen Trail as it dips down to a gate at the park boundary. At the next gate, there's a stile. Turn right and climb open ground to the fire tower atop the hill with outstanding views of nearby peaks. Drop south from the summit and veer right off the vehicle track to look for a stile and marker post that lead you back into the scrub. Continue along a fence beside a pine plantation. At the fence end, turn right onto the fire track that narrows to a foot trail. This eases down rocky ground to rejoin the track leading from Watts Gully Rd. Hit Bar 41 (41 Queen St) in Williamstown for your post-walk snacks.

**55**

**Location**
60km north-east from Adelaide

**Distance**
9km return

**Grade**
Hard

**Ideal Season**
Autumn

**Notes**
No dogs
Track unsealed
Steep terrain

Photo: Warren Conservation Park
© Paul Weston

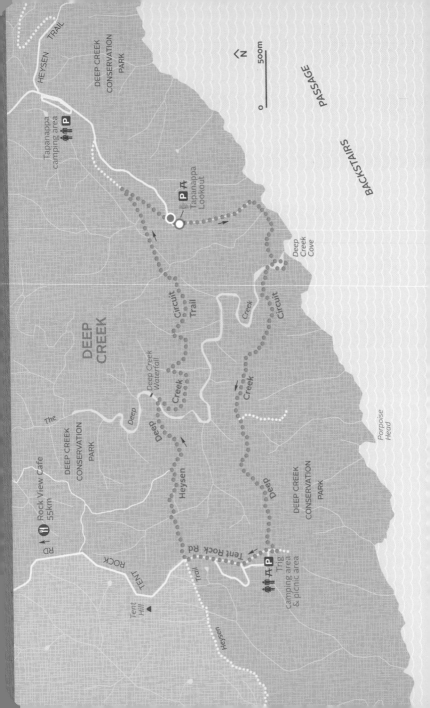

# DEEP CREEK CIRCUIT
## DEEP CREEK CONSERVATION PARK

**56**

Ambitious circuit navigating rugged coves, waterfalls and sharp ridges – all against a backdrop of dramatic coastal and island scenery.

From Tapanappa Lookout, take the track to Deep Creek Cove dropping south to the coast. Head west along the coast; the path narrows and dips to a rocky cove. Continue to climb onto the next ridge and then edge carefully down another steep rib with expansive gorge views upstream. Deep Creek Cove below has a shingle beach and secluded sand-banked estuary by which to relax. Cross the creek – take care after heavy rains – and climb the long rising spur through thick scrub to Trig camping area. Follow Tent Rock Rd north for approximately 1km and then turn right to join the Heysen Trail. The track winds eastward through steep woodland down to the shady confines of Deep Creek Waterfall. Follow the track downstream where it contours back up to higher ground and Tapanappa's wonderful ridge top. Refuel at Rock View Cafe (1 Mt Alma Rd, Inman Valley).

**Location**
100km south-west from Adelaide

**Distance**
10.9km circuit

**Grade**
Hard

**Ideal Season**
Autumn

**Notes**
No dogs
Track unsealed
Steep terrain

Photo: Sunrise from Tapanappa Lookout
© Quentin Chester

Adelaide

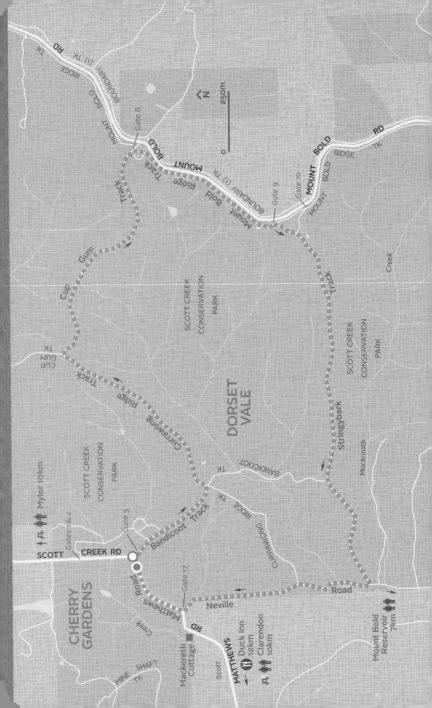

# SCOTT CREEK
## SCOTT CREEK CONSERVATION PARK

Loop walk exploring a mix of bush and grassy woodland tucked deep within the Mt Lofty Ranges. This woodland is a stronghold for the southern brown bandicoot. Though nocturnal, bandicoots and the yellow-footed antechinus are sometimes spotted during the day in the winter months.

From Gate 3 on Scott Creek Rd head up Bandicoot Track. Turn left at the junction with Currawong Ridge Track. Follow this for a kilometre and turn right onto Cup Gum Track – a climb rewarded with views to the southern vales. At the top of the ridge turn right and follow the fenceline beside Mt Bold Rd. From the next intersection turn right down Stringybark Track as it slips into a sheltered gully – prime bandicoot habitat. Turn right onto Neville Rd. Follow this to Matthews Rd – near the site of a handsome cottage built by the Mackereth family in 1840 – and turn right again back to Gate 3. Warm up with pub nosh and open fires at Coromandel Valley's Duck Inn (393 Main Rd).

**57**

**Location**
28km south from Adelaide

**Distance**
7km circuit

**Grade**
Easy

**Ideal Season**
Winter

**Map**
UBD 168 H16

**Notes**
No dogs
Track unsealed

Photo: Southern brown bandicoot, Scott Creek Conservation Park
© Kerry Schneider

Adelaide

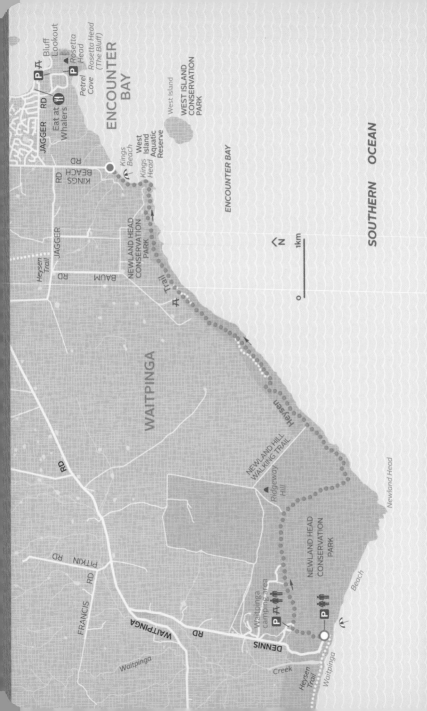

# WAITPINGA BEACH TO KINGS HEAD
## NEWLAND HEAD CONSERVATION PARK

Impressive cliff-top walk with stunning wild vistas of beaches, open ocean and islands, plus the chance of whale and rare seabird sightings.

From the carpark at the eastern end of Waitpinga Beach, head up past the campground and onto the wide sandy track climbing inland to the crown of Newland Head Conservation Park. The route then veers southeast and dips gently towards the coast and the cliffs. The remainder of the walk edges through coastal mallee scrub atop these dark, steeply tilted slabs. White-bellied sea eagles and peregrine falcons are occasionally spotted along this stretch. Wind-pruned heath and twisted mallees display the power of the Southern Ocean; so too the wave-washed granite forms of West Island and the Bluff. The final stages of the walk ease down from the cliff-tops to the rocky prow of Kings Head. Then it's a short beach stroll to the end of Kings Beach Rd. Grab a bite – and more views – at Eat at Whalers (121 Franklin Pde), near the Bluff.

**Location**
91km south from Adelaide

**Distance**
10.5km one way

**Grade**
Medium

**Ideal Season**
Winter

**Notes**
No dogs
Track unsealed
Exposed
cliff-tops

Photo: Looking from Waitpinga Cliffs to the Bluff
© Quentin Chester

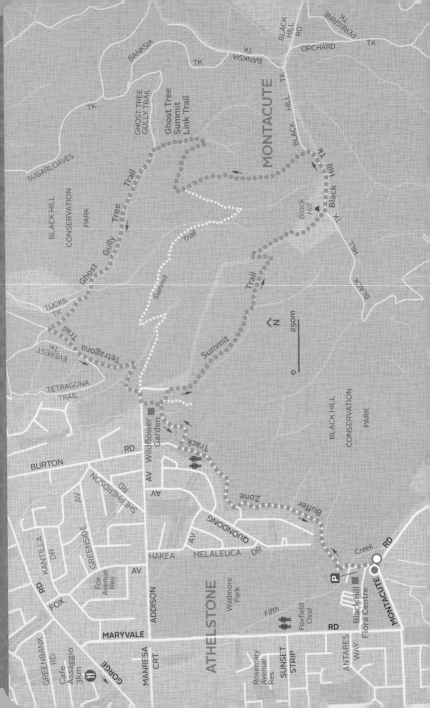

# BLACK HILL SUMMIT
## BLACK HILL CONSERVATION PARK

Vigorous circuit taking in gullies and high ridges with a diverse mix of woodland, on the hills overlooking Adelaide's east.

From the park's Maryvale Rd entrance, head towards the Wildflower Garden following the Buffer Zone Track. After visiting the gardens, turn right to join the Summit Trail. A stiff climb leads up through a mosaic of vegetation, including grass trees, heathland plants and low sheoaks. Continue on high ground, turning left at the intersection with the Black Hill Track. After around 500m, turn right onto the Ghost Tree Summit Link Trail as it twists down to join the main Ghost Tree Gully Trail. Mooch down this sheltered valley to the intersection with the Tetragona Trail. Turn left and follow this to the end of Addison Ave. About 100m down the avenue, turn left to pass through the Wildflower Garden. Turn right to rejoin the Buffer Zone Track and go back to the carpark near Maryvale Rd. Sample the Italian fare at Cafe Assaggio (84 Newton Rd).

59

**Location**
12km north-east from Adelaide

**Distance**
8km circuit

**Grade**
Hard

**Ideal Season**
Winter

**Map**
UBD 108 N8

**Notes**
No dogs
Track unsealed
Steep ascent

Photo: *Hakea prostrata* has masses of highly scented flowers in late winter / early spring
© Bill Doyle

Adelaide

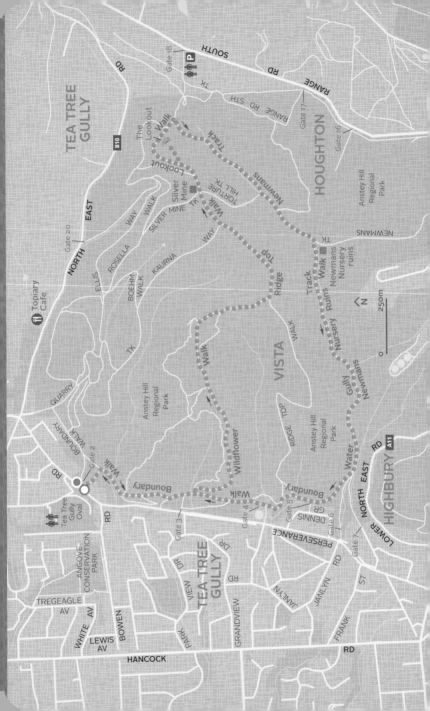

# ANSTEY HILL
## ANSTEY HILL RECREATION PARK

Hilltop and woodland ramble offering sweeping views of Adelaide's north-east fringe, together with relics from the area's early mining and farming days. Along the way there are a couple of side trips. The first visits an old silver mine, a vertical shaft sunk in 1888. The second detour takes in a lookout with panoramic vistas of the park and beyond.

Enter the park from Gate 2 on Perseverance Rd, then turn right to follow the Boundary Walk. After 500m, head left onto the Wildflower Walk and climb to the crest of the ridge. At the top turn left onto the Ridge Top Walk, where you can take a side trip. Back on the main track, take the Lookout Walk dropping to the junction with Newmans Track. This leads down to the Water Gully Track, past the historic site of Newmans Nursery. Dating from 1854, these orchards once formed part of the largest nursery in the southern hemisphere. At the junction with the Boundary Walk veer right and follow this back to the start of the walk. To see the latter-day Newman's Nursery visit the Topiary Cafe (1361 North East Rd).

60

**Location**
19km north-east
from Adelaide

**Distance**
7.5km circuit

**Grade**
Medium

**Ideal Season**
Winter

**Map**
UBD 85 G13

**Notes**
Dogs permitted
Track unsealed

Adelaide
***
135

Photo: Newmans Nursery
© Natalie Townsend

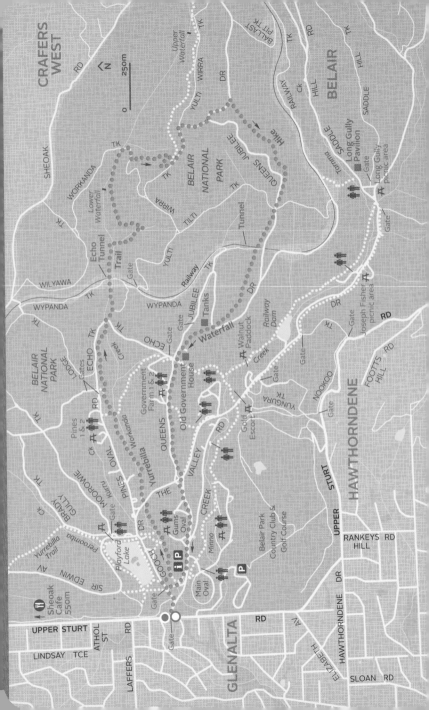

# BELAIR WATERFALLS
## BELAIR NATIONAL PARK

Loop walk venturing into the upper reaches of this beloved bush playground – Australia's second National Park.

**61**

From the carpark inside the main gate take the Echo Tunnel Track. Beyond a small bridge, the path eases through blue gums alongside Workanda Creek. The trail crosses a fire track before heading into the 50m-long Echo Tunnel – take care on the rocks if the creek is flowing. Just beyond the tunnel head right up onto the ridge and follow Workanda Track past Lower Waterfall. Veer right onto a link track that winds down to cross Yulti Wirra Track and Queens Jubilee Dr. Continue uphill past the old lookout. An old vehicle track leads downhill to an intersection with Queens Jubilee Dr and Tilti Track. Cross over and drop down past tanks to Old Government House. From here a footpath beside Queens Jubilee Dr sidles downhill to the main gate. Back along Upper Sturt Rd, enjoy a coffee and snack at Sheoak Cafe (38 Sheoak Rd).

**Location**
13km south-east from Adelaide

**Distance**
7km return

**Grade**
Medium

**Ideal Season**
Spring

**Map**
UBD 143 D15

**Notes**
Track sealed and unsealed
Take a torch for Echo Tunnel

Photo: Upper Waterfall
© Stuart Holden

Adelaide

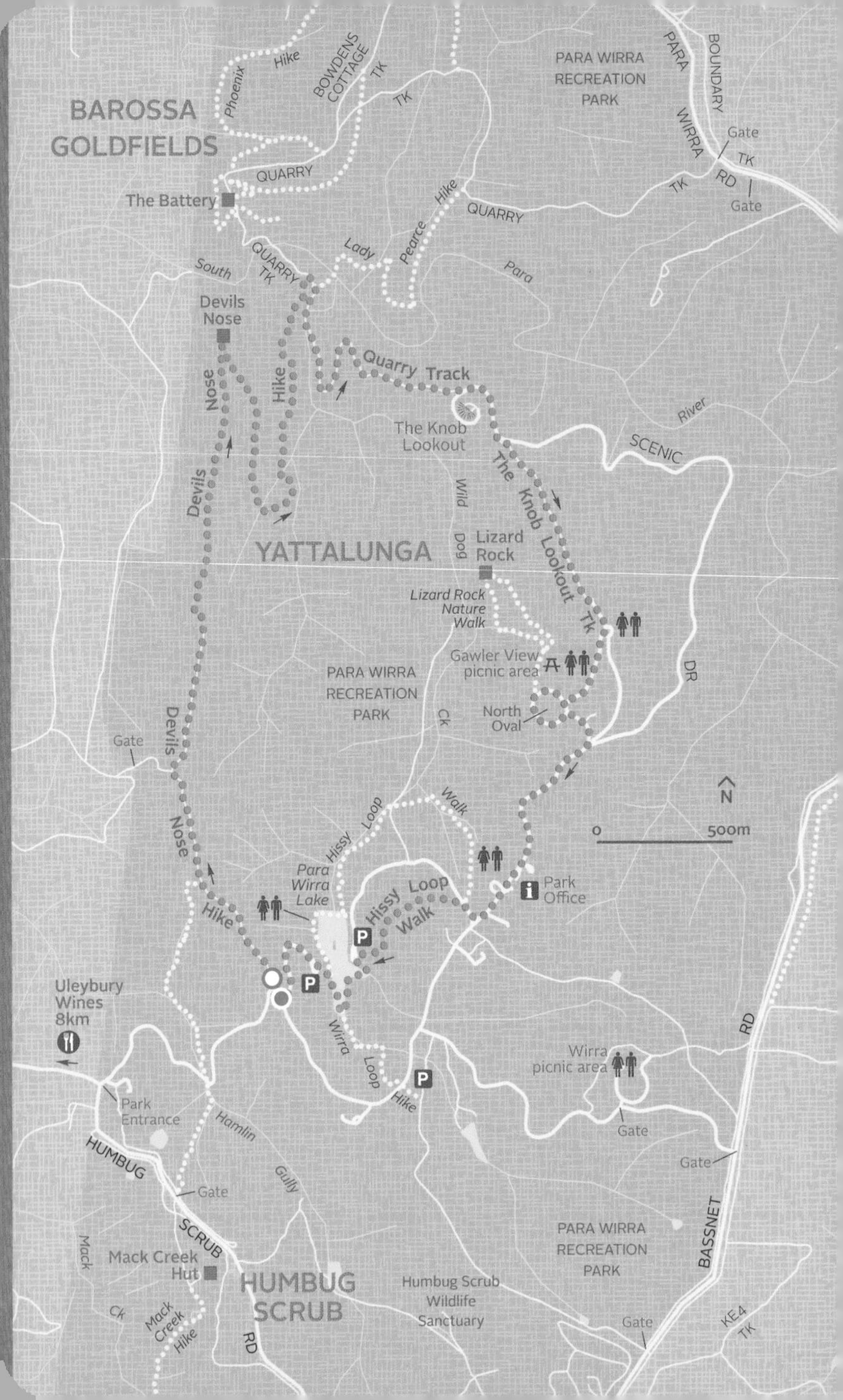

BAROSSA
GOLDFIELDS

PARA WIRRA
RECREATION
PARK

Phoenix Hike

BOWDENS COTTAGE TK

TK

PARA WIRRA RD

BOUNDARY

Gate
TK

QUARRY

Lady

Pearce Hike

QUARRY

Gate

TK

The Battery

South

QUARRY TK

Para

Nose Hike

Devils Nose

Devils Nose Hike

Quarry Track

The Knob
Lookout

SCENIC

River

YATTALUNGA

Wild Dog

Lizard Rock

The Knob Lookout Tk

Lizard Rock
Nature Walk

Gawler View
picnic area

DR

PARA WIRRA
RECREATION
PARK

Ck

North Oval

Gate

Devils Nose Hike

Walk

Hissy Loop

Para
Wirra Lake

Hissy Loop Walk

Park
Office

i

Wirra
picnic area

P

Uleybury Wines
8km

P

P

Wirra Loop Hike

P

Gate

Park
Entrance

Hamlin

Gate

HUMBUG

Gully

SCRUB RD

Mack

Mack Creek Hut

Mack Creek Hike

Ck

HUMBUG
SCRUB

Humbug Scrub
Wildlife
Sanctuary

PARA WIRRA
RECREATION
PARK

Gate

Gate

BASSNET RD

KE4 TK

N

0          500m

# PARA WIRRA

## PARA WIRRA CONSERVATION PARK

Accessible, ridge-top wander delivering sweeping views north towards the South Para River, Barossa Ranges and beyond.

From the Devils Nose carpark on the lake's western side, take the Devils Nose Track heading north along the ridge with outcrops of ancient sandstone. It's a short side-trip to the lookout spectacle from atop the Nose. The main track then swings down through big stands of grass trees *(Xanthorrhoea)* to the base of the gorge along Wild Dog Creek. At the bottom, take the Knob Lookout Track on the right that climbs out of the gorge to deliver more valley views at the lookout. Continue along the Knob Lookout Track as it heads south-east to a gate and then weaves around the ovals, picnic areas and tennis courts. Looping around the North Oval, turn right onto the sealed road. Follow this past the park office, then 200m down the road, turn right to skirt around the lake to the western side and the trailhead. On weekends grab a wood-fired oven pizza at nearby Uleybury Wines (Uley Rd).

**62**

**Location**
40km north-east from Adelaide

**Distance**
9km circuit

**Grade**
Easy

**Ideal Season**
Spring

**Notes**
No dogs
Track unsealed
Exposed
cliff-tops

Photo: Lake at Para Wirra
© Jeff Lusher

Adelaide

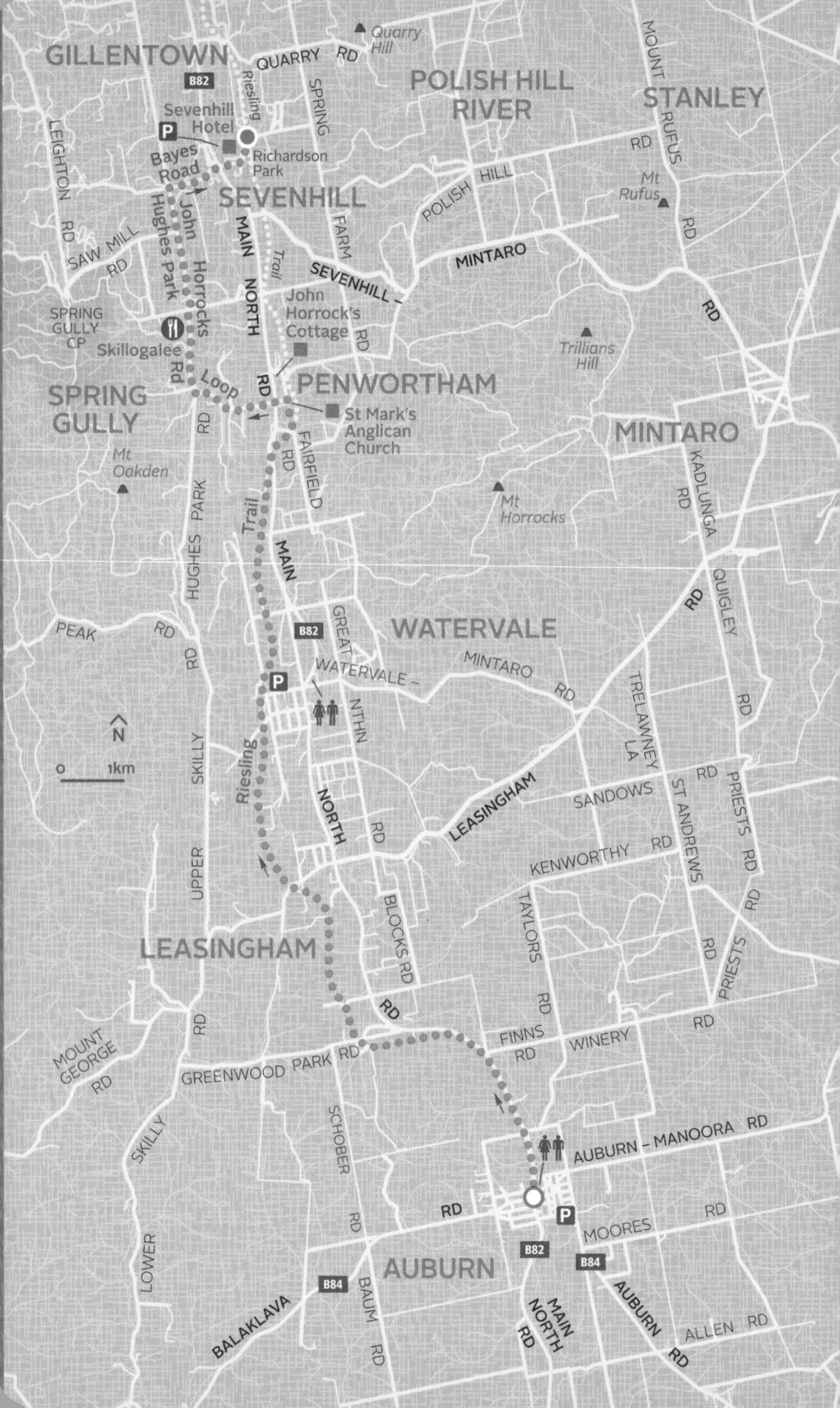
GILLENTOWN
QUARRY RD
Quarry Hill
POLISH HILL RIVER
STANLEY
MOUNT RUFUS RD
B82
Riesling Trail
SPRING FARM RD
Sevenhill Hotel
Richardson Park
Bayes Road
SEVENHILL
LEIGHTON RD
POLISH HILL RD
Mt Rufus
SAW MILL RD
John Hughes Park
John Horrocks Loop
MAIN NORTH RD
MINTARO
SEVENHILL – MINTARO RD
John Horrock's Cottage
SPRING GULLY CP
Skillogalee Rd
Trillians Hill
SPRING GULLY
PENWORTHAM
St Mark's Anglican Church
MINTARO
Mt Oakden
FAIRFIELD RD
Mt Horrocks
KADLUNGA RD
HUGHES PARK RD
QUIGLEY RD
WATERVALE
PEAK RD
GREAT NTHN RD
WATERVALE – MINTARO RD
TRELAWNEY LA
N
0 1km
SKILLY RD
UPPER SKILLY RD
LEASINGHAM RD
SANDOWS RD
ST ANDREWS RD
PRIESTS RD
KENWORTHY RD
BLOCKS RD
TAYLORS RD
LEASINGHAM
FINNS RD
WINERY RD
MOUNT GEORGE RD
GREENWOOD PARK RD
AUBURN – MANOORA RD
SCHOBER RD
MOORES RD
AUBURN
B84
BALAKLAVA RD
BAUM RD
LOWER SKILLY RD
AUBURN RD
ALLEN RD

# RIESLING TRAIL
## CLARE VALLEY

Wondrous trail that drifts among the vineyards, historic towns and farm country perched in the rambling woodland of the Clare Valley. This is the heart of Riesling country with cellar doors aplenty for sampling the valley's exquisite expressions of this grape variety.

The trail sidles – with many potential diversions – along the old Riverton to Spalding railway line. This section covers the stretch from the townships of Auburn to Sevenhill, both of which boast a rich history. Walking north, the trail passes through tree-lined paddocks and vineyards on its way to Leasingham and then Watervale. Head west from Penwortham past St Mark's Anglican Church to detour along the John Horrocks Loop – home to some of the region's stellar food and wine haunts dotted in the rolling hinterland above Hughes Park Rd. Linger if you can over the renowned local fare at Skillogalee (Trevarrick Rd). The loop brings you back down to Sevenhill via Bayes Rd and the town's famed pub.

**63**

**Location**
130km north from Adelaide

**Distance**
20km return

**Grade**
Easy

**Ideal Season**
Spring

**Notes**
Dogs permitted
Track sealed
and unsealed

Photo: Vineyards in the Clare Valley
© Tony Macrellis

Adelaide

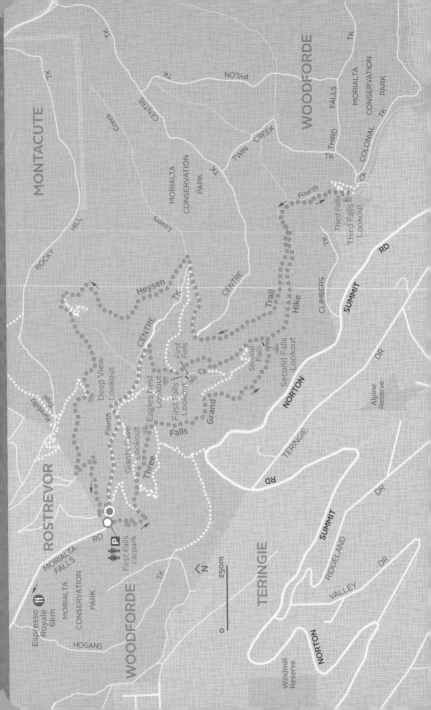

# MORIALTA GORGE
## MORIALTA CONSERVATION PARK

64

Loop walk taking in the three main waterfalls in this dramatic, crag-lined ravine – a hidden, yet accessible, gem of the Adelaide Hills. The cliff-top views of the gorge and out across the city beyond are spectacular – it's almost hard to believe this grand gulch is so close to town.

From the First Falls carpark take the Three Falls Grand Hike that works its way along the southern side of the gorge. There are great outlooks along the way. Above the First Falls, the track continues along the shaded course of Fourth Creek to visit both the Second and Third falls. From the Third Falls retrace your steps back downstream and turn right to take the continuation of the Three Falls Grand Hike. The track contours along high ground above the long gullies and spurs on the gorge's northern flanks. From the lofty perch of the Deep View Lookout the track skirts the cliff-tops before zigzagging back downhill to the First Falls carpark. Try Espresso Royale (357 Magill Rd) for a caffeine boost on the way home.

**Location**
12km east from Adelaide

**Distance**
8km circuit

**Grade**
Medium

**Ideal Season**
Spring

**Map**
UBD 108 N16

**Notes**
No dogs
Track unsealed
Exposed cliff-tops

Photo: Panorama of Morialta Conservation Park showing the gorge and First Falls
© Peter Neaum via Wikimedia Commons

Adelaide

143

# PERTH
## WESTERN AUSTRALIA

Beach, bush, river and hills – walkers in and around Perth are spoilt for choice. Add to this an enticing Mediterranean-style climate and there's no reason not to venture outdoors at every given opportunity.

Start your exploration of the city along the Swan River. Lined with forest, it passes spectacular Kings Park and Botanic Garden, home to a feast of natives, including many of the wildflowers for which south-west WA is famed, as well as a gigantic 750-year-old boab that was transplanted from the Kimberley, 3000km to the north.

Where the river runs into the sea you'll find glittering water views – follow the trails here as they pass seasonal sculptures and along sweeping strands of sand before cooling off in the aquamarine embrace of the Indian Ocean.

In East Perth, join the Pilgrim Trail. Forged in centuries past, it winds 160km north to the monastic town of New Norcia, established in the 1840s by Benedictine monks. Head further east into the hills and you'll discover historic railway lines, granite gorges, meandering streams, tumbling waterfalls and impressive stands of jarrah.

The city is also a great stepping off point for the 1000km Bibbulmun Track, which winds from Perth to Albany, on WA's south coast. It's a spectacular walking trail that dances through mighty forests of marri, along windswept coastlines and over mountainsides spread with wildflowers. You won't want to miss it.

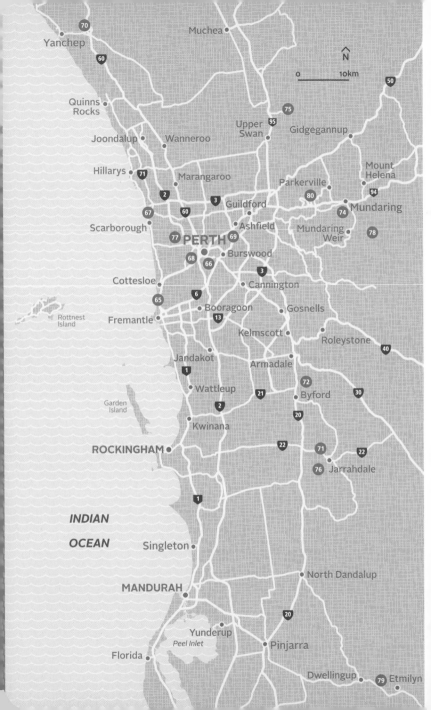

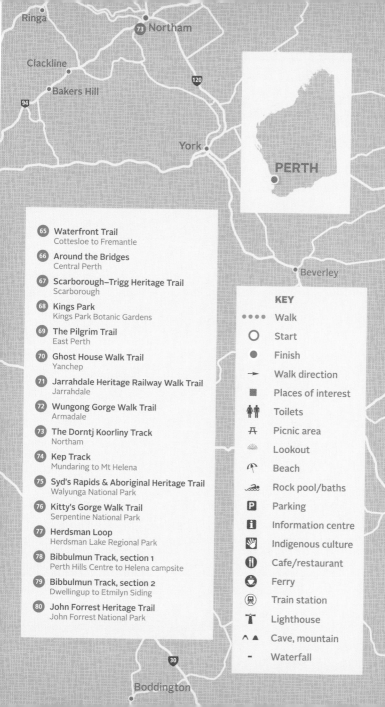

Ringa

Northam 73

Clackline

120

Bakers Hill

94

York

PERTH

Beverley

65 **Waterfront Trail**
Cottesloe to Fremantle

66 **Around the Bridges**
Central Perth

67 **Scarborough–Trigg Heritage Trail**
Scarborough

68 **Kings Park**
Kings Park Botanic Gardens

69 **The Pilgrim Trail**
East Perth

70 **Ghost House Walk Trail**
Yanchep

71 **Jarrahdale Heritage Railway Walk Trail**
Jarrahdale

72 **Wungong Gorge Walk Trail**
Armadale

73 **The Dorntj Koorliny Track**
Northam

74 **Kep Track**
Mundaring to Mt Helena

75 **Syd's Rapids & Aboriginal Heritage Trail**
Walyunga National Park

76 **Kitty's Gorge Walk Trail**
Serpentine National Park

77 **Herdsman Loop**
Herdsman Lake Regional Park

78 **Bibbulmun Track, section 1**
Perth Hills Centre to Helena campsite

79 **Bibbulmun Track, section 2**
Dwellingup to Etmilyn Siding

80 **John Forrest Heritage Trail**
John Forrest National Park

**KEY**

●●●● Walk

○ Start

● Finish

→ Walk direction

▦ Places of interest

👫 Toilets

⊼ Picnic area

�▨ Lookout

⛱ Beach

🏊 Rock pool/baths

P Parking

ℹ Information centre

✋ Indigenous culture

🍴 Cafe/restaurant

⚓ Ferry

🚉 Train station

⊤ Lighthouse

∧ ▲ Cave, mountain

– Waterfall

30

Boddington

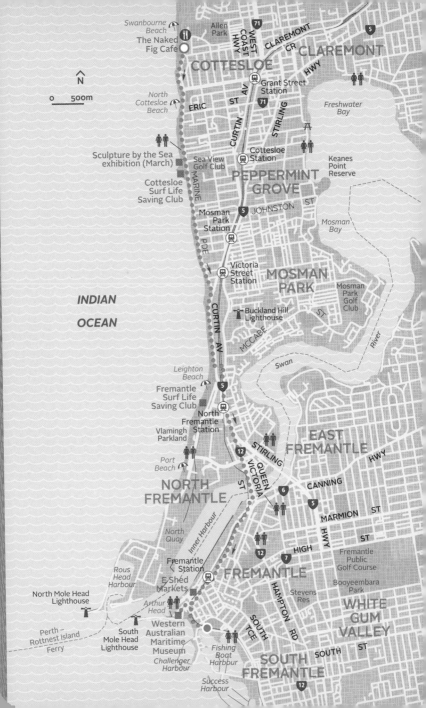

# WATERFRONT TRAIL
## COTTESLOE TO FREMANTLE

Trail passes some of WA's most stunning ocean frontages taking in glittering water, breweries and even Bon Scott.

Power up with a coffee at the Naked Fig Cafe (278 Marine Pde, Swanbourne) then walk uphill with the Indian Ocean to your right. From the top of the hill, the path remains straight and flat all the way to Fremantle. You'll pass numerous sculptures from Cottesloe Beach's annual Sculpture by the Sea exhibition (March). Dazzling ocean views continue as the path veers away from Marine Pde through coastal scrub, then sidles up to Curtin Ave. As you approach a circular grassed area at Leighton Beach, take the public laneway through the luxury apartment complex, cross Curtin Ave and follow the path through North Fremantle Station. Turn right onto Stirling Hwy, then Queen Victoria St. Continue over the bridge, following the harbourside footpath to reach Fremantle Station. Rounding the station, make for the E Shed markets then continue on to the Maritime Museum. After your visit, double back towards the markets, turning right at the Port Authority. Find the path along the railway and pass Fremantle's historic buildings. Spy the sculpture of Bon Scott at the Fishing Boat Harbour.

**65**

**Location**
12.4km south from Perth

**Distance**
10km one way

**Grade**
Easy

**Ideal Season**
Summer

**Map**
UBD 285 Q8

**Notes**
Dogs allowed on leash
Track sealed and unsealed
Shared path

Photo: Cottesloe Beach
© Ryan Williams

Perth

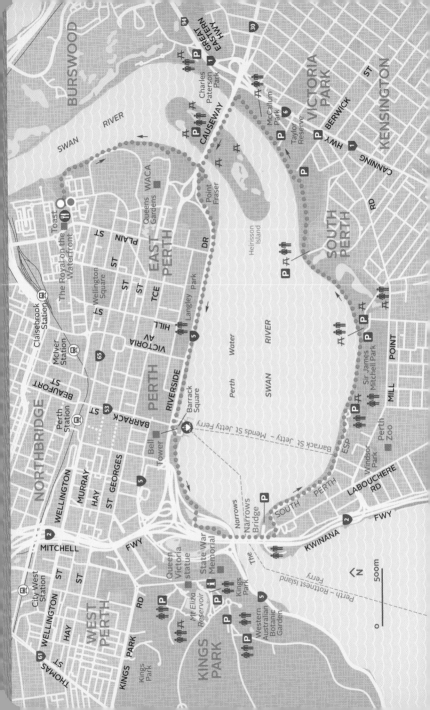

# AROUND THE BRIDGES
## CENTRAL PERTH

City walk clutching Perth's Swan River and delivering city skyscraper panoramas from two distinct, and beautiful, grassy angles. Consider walking at dusk, when the city lights create a beautiful reflection in the river.

Start your journey with a bite at Toast (60 Royal St, East Perth), overlooking Claisebrook Cove. Head east, keeping the inlet on your left as it merges with Swan River. Turn right and walk along the riverside. Duck under the Causeway Bridge and keep on the walk/cycle path as it joins Riverside Dr. Enjoy the views of the CBD along this straight, flat stretch. Reach Barrack Sq where you can take a shortcut on a ferry across to South Perth, or explore the Bell Tower. Otherwise, follow the path until you reach an underpass on your right. Take it, following the curve around a small lake, through another underpass and along another lake. Go over the Narrows Bridge, exit and cross Mill Point Rd then walk along the Esplanade, catching stunning city views. The ferry jetty is at the end of Mends St. Walk along the waterfront to the Causeway. Cross the bridge to return to your starting point. Finish with a tipple at the Royal on the Waterfront (60 Royal St, East Perth).

**66**

**Location**
1km south from Perth

**Distance**
13.5km circuit

**Grade**
Easy

**Ideal Season**
Summer

**Map**
UBD 3 C8

**Notes**
Dogs permitted
Shortcut with a ferry

Photo: Black swans on the Swan River
© P. Elliott

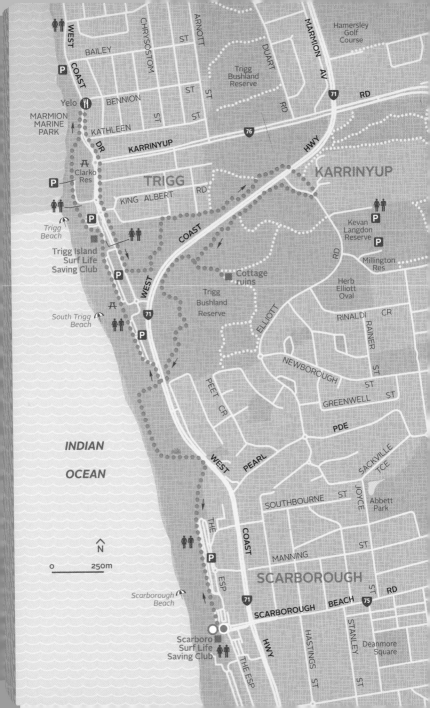

# SCARBOROUGH–TRIGG HERITAGE TRAIL
## SCARBOROUGH

Sand, surf and scrub combine along this popular track through native tea tree, wattle and tuart (gum).

From Scarboro Surf Life Saving Club on the Esplanade, cross the amphitheatre and go up the adjacent ramp. Take the steps to the bicycle path, walking northwards; arrows show the way. Continue along Scarborough Beach and veer onto West Coast Hwy until the path turns towards the ocean, passing a lookout: enjoy views of Rottnest Island. Stroll along the seashore towards Trigg Beach. Once you reach another sign, take a sharp right turn towards the highway. Follow the pathway's S-bend before clutching the coast again. Continue past Trigg Island Surf Life Saving Club and Clarko Reserve, then follow West Coast Dr to the corner of Bennion St and visit Yelo (331 West Coast Dr, Trigg), a breakfast haven. Head south on the east side; an arrow directs you to Trigg Bushland Reserve. Follow the limestone trail through the underpass at West Coast Hwy and turn right at the next sign. Continue straight ahead as the track curls left through Rottnest cypresses. It snakes to an underpass, returning you to Scarborough Beach.

**67**

**Location**
12km north-west from Perth

**Distance**
7.8km circuit

**Grade**
Medium

**Ideal Season**
Summer

**Map**
UBD 245 Q3

**Notes**
Dogs allowed on leash
Track sealed and unsealed
Interpretative signage
Beware snakes in bushland

Photo: Footsteps in the sand
© Simon Burrows Photography

# KINGS PARK
## KINGS PARK BOTANIC GARDENS

The pride of Perth, this scenic track takes in the city's Botanic Gardens, 291 different species of native plants and a spectacular walkway above the treetops.

From the visitor centre, follow the signs to the Lotterywest Federation Walkway. With superb views of the city, it stretches 620m through the Botanic Garden along a mix of pathways and an elevated 52m glass-and-steel arched bridge suspended among a canopy of eucalypts: admire the pylons, rusted to match the surrounding bush and covered in plant motifs. At the walkway's end, follow the signs for Roe Gardens, taking a left turn to reach Forrest Dr. Turn right and walk until you reach Fire Fighters Memorial Gr. For more fantastic views, climb 15m DNA Tower before heading down the Broadwalk, crossing Lovekin Dr and making your way to Synergy Parkland. Stop at Zamia Cafe (May Dr) for the delicious field mushroom and herb rice pilaf. Skirting the lake, cross May Dr, turn right and follow the path past the Saw Ave picnic area before taking the left-hand path. After 500m, take the right-hand turn and continue on to Lotterywest Family Area and beyond it Pines Picnic Area, then return to your starting point.

**68**

**Location**
Central Perth

**Distance**
7km circuit

**Grade**
Easy

**Ideal Season**
Summer

**Map**
UBD 1 G15

**Notes**
No dogs
Track sealed
Fantastic city
and river views

Photo: Lotterywest Federation Walkway, Kings Park
© Rakesh Agrawal

Perth

# THE PILGRIM TRAIL
## EAST PERTH

Leg one of a historic trail along the Camino Salvado: a 160km trail which starts in Perth and ends at the New Norcia monastery.

Cross the bridge over Claisebrook Cove in East Perth. Stick to the waterfront and follow the Swan River. Head under Windan Bridge and continue on the tree-lined trail. After Bardon Park, the route turns right and crosses East St. Continue through Berringa Reserve, staying on the path parallel to Woodhouse Rd, then turn left onto Fogerthorpe Cres, which becomes Richard St. Turn left again on Swan View Tce; when you hit a Y-junction, take the right-hand branch and return to the foreshore. Stroll through the Baigup wetlands en route to the carpark at Bayswater Paddlesports Club, returning you to the riverside path. Go right at the T-junction, taking the underpass beneath Tonkin Hwy. Veer right to the waterfront, and turn left at the jetty. The track eventually heads north along West Rd and then Bassendean Pde, which turns into North Rd. Cross the bridge at Guildford Rd, staying on this street and refuelling at the Lounge Room (187 James St). At the Johnson St traffic lights, cross the train tracks. Finish your walk at St Matthew's Anglican Church.

**69**

Location
1km east from
Perth

Distance
14km one way

Grade
Easy

Ideal Season
Autumn

Map
UBD 3 C8

Notes
Dogs allowed
on leash
Trail markers

Photo: Claisebrook Cove
© Simon Burrows Photography

Perth

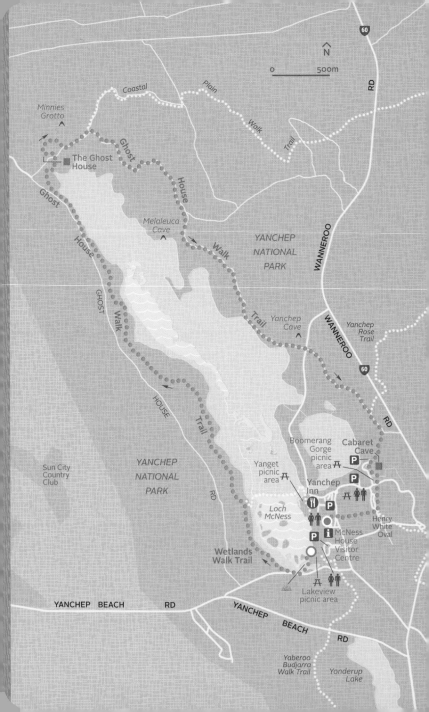

# GHOST HOUSE WALK TRAIL

## YANCHEP

Nature-lovers' trail taking in native bush land replete with koalas, kangaroos and elegant water birds.

Depart from the Lakeview picnic area with the coastal wetland, Loch McNess, on your right. From the viewing platform, look for waterbirds – coots, pelicans and darters – through the bulrushes. Follow the Wetlands Walk Trail until the Ghosthouse Walk Trail branches off to the left; then venture into the native wilderness. About halfway along this 9.2km stretch, check out the remains of 'The Ghost House' (built in the early 1900s); an old cottage that inspired the trail's name. Further on, a spur in the trail leads to a rammed-earth shelter, which is used by overnight walkers. When you come to Cabaret Cave, join the Yanchep Rose Walk, which winds through Boomerang Gorge picnic area and past Henry White Oval. Follow it back to the parking lot, turn right and make a beeline for the historic Yanchep Inn (3499 Wanneroo Rd, Yanchep National Park). Stop here for great food and a rest in the company of kangaroos. Return via the Koala Boardwalk to McNess House visitor centre, just near your starting point.

70

**Location**
51km north from Perth

**Distance**
11.2km circuit

**Grade**
Medium

**Ideal Season**
Autumn

**Map**
UBD 44 A10

**Notes**
No dogs
Trail markers
Entry fees
apply

Photo: Yanchep National Park
© Zoe Fletcher

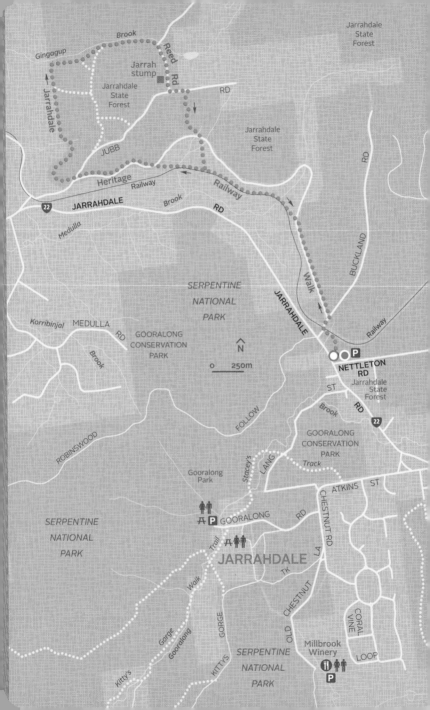

# JARRAHDALE HERITAGE RAILWAY WALK TRAIL

## JARRAHDALE

Bush trail following 1872 railway line, which carted timber from local mills to the port of Rockingham, where it was shipped overseas.

Set off from the carpark on the corner of Nettleton and Jarrahdale rds; the latter, like the nearby town, is named after the jarrah trees that grow there. Trace the train track, crossing at Buckland Rd. Walk on, watching out for the sharp left turn down a single-file path, which leads you to a gravel road alongside a modern railway. From here you'll score fabulous views of the coast. Veer right back to the historic railway and follow the tracks west until you reach Jubb Rd. Cross and enter a wandoo woodland. Curve right, then left, through kangaroo grass and further along climb uphill alongside jarrah and marri trees. At the granite outcrop, veer right along Gingagup Brook, where there are huge tree ferns. At the second bridge, turn right along Reed Rd and stop at a jarrah stump with a peg – dating back to the 1800s – embedded in the trunk. On Jubb Rd, take a sharp right to the track where grass trees grow and head downhill. Return to your starting point. Visit Millbrook Winery (Old Chestnut La) for seasonal fare sourced from its garden.

**71**

**Location**
50km south-east from Perth

**Distance**
7km circuit

**Grade**
Medium

**Ideal Season**
Autumn

**Map**
UBD 483 K2

**Notes**
No dogs
One short rocky ascent
Trail markers

Photo: Jarrahdale
© Lee Davis

Perth

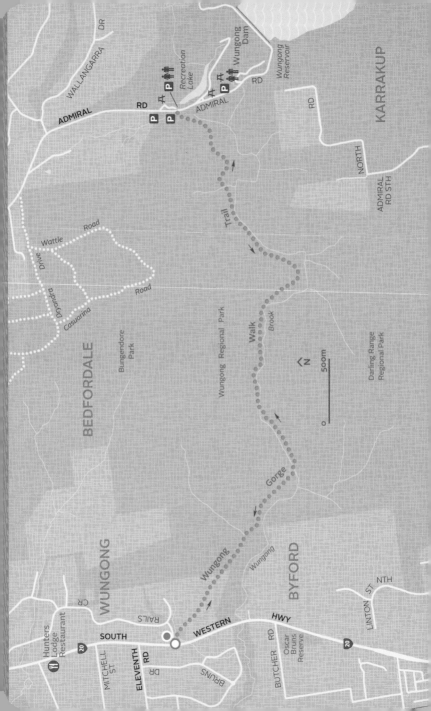

# WUNGONG GORGE WALK TRAIL
## ARMADALE

## 72

Weaving trail through Wungong Regional Park, along granite gorges and beside a meandering stream.

Start by the South Western Hwy, about 200m south of Rails Cres, where there's a small, grassed area. Follow the dirt trail south-east through the scrub as it mirrors Wungong Brook, which cuts through the heart of the gorge. Spy the remains of an old granite quarry; its mined rock was used to build the Garden Island causeway, across from Rockingham. As you head into the granite gorges, look for magpies, eagles, galahs and kangaroos as well as the ruins of a cottage. Continue through native jarrah and marri forest as the gorge walls grow taller. There are optional climbs out of the gorge on either side (about 200m each) if you're keen to chase impressive views of the gorge and the Swan Coastal Plain. Continue along the brook as it snakes towards Admiral Rd, where you'll find a picnic area and plenty of amenities (a second car could be left here to shorten the walk). Return the way you came and head north up the South Western Hwy to Hunters Lodge Restaurant (7 Moore St) for an early dinner.

**Location**
33km south-east from Perth

**Distance**
12km return

**Grade**
Hard

**Ideal Season**
Autumn

**Map**
UBD 412 K5

**Notes**
No dogs
Uphill climbs
Native wildlife

Photo: Drumstick Isopogon Inflorescence
© Ian Wallace

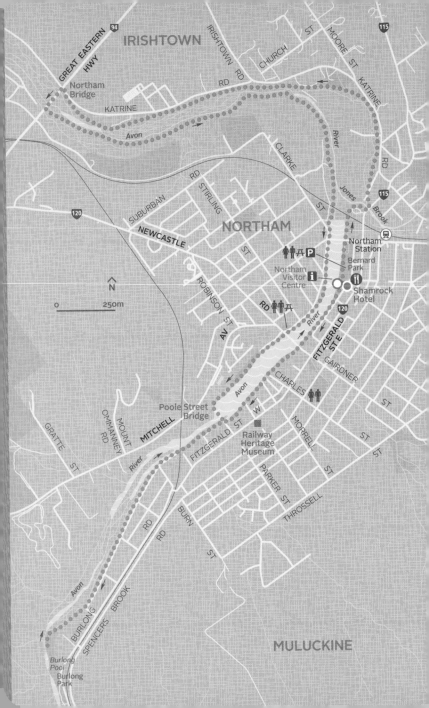

# THE DORNTJ KOORLINY TRACK

## NORTHAM

Scenic circuit with a taste of local Aboriginal heritage, quaint footbridges, abundant birdlife and, with luck, inquisitive echidnas. 'Dorntj Koorliny' is Noongar for walking together.

Walk south-west from the Northam visitor centre, keeping the Avon River on your right. Continue ambling upstream, noting the Poole St Bridge, crossing the train tracks and, 4.5km from your departure point, reaching Burlong Park. This is a lovely picnic spot with rich Aboriginal heritage – the interpretative signage tells of the local Noongar people. Retrace your steps, and on your way consider visiting the Railway Heritage Museum. Behind the visitor centre, duck in for lunch at the charming Shamrock Hotel (112 Fitzgerald St), built in 1866. Follow the river downstream as it heads towards the Great Eastern Hwy, crossing at Peel Tce and following the narrower waterway until it reaches Katrine Rd. Keep going before crossing the highway to the other side of the river. Follow the track upstream again, sticking to the riverbanks and heading back into town. If you're lucky, you may see echidnas. Once you reach Poole St Bridge, return to the visitor centre.

**73**

**Location**
96km east from Perth

**Distance**
18km circuit

**Grade**
Medium

**Ideal Season**
Winter

**Notes**
Dogs permitted
Passes several pubs
Footprint track markers
Interpretative signage

Photo: Echidna
© Wayne Butterworth

Perth

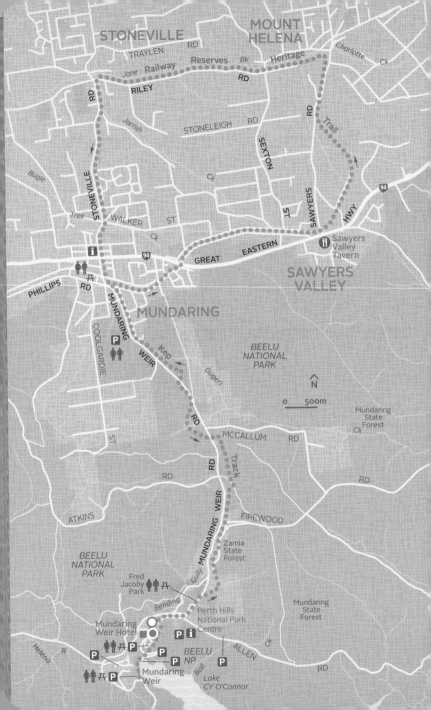

# KEP TRACK
## MUNDARING TO MT HELENA

Part one of 75km Kep Track, taking in a section of the ground-breaking Perth–Kalgoorlie Eastern Goldfields pipeline.

From Mundaring Weir Hotel, take the Weir Walk track across the dam wall, scoring awesome water and forest views. Return past No. 1 Pump Station and back along the pipeline to the hotel. Take the Kep Track, which nudges Mundaring Weir Rd. It follows part of CY O'Connor's remarkable pipeline, built in the 1890s to supply water to Kalgoorlie. Kep is a Noongar word for water. You'll pass a picnic area in Fred Jacoby Park and see pipeline along the way. Arrive at Sculpture Park, near the visitor centre, and take some time to explore. Continue along Kep Track and cross the Great Eastern Hwy, past the cemetery, between Railway and Helena tces. You're now passing through Sawyers Valley, named for its timber-cutting history. Refuel at Sawyers Valley Tavern (10860 Great Eastern Hwy) before heading uphill to Mt Helena along Sawyers Rd. Turn west along the old Rail Reserve Heritage Trail to return to Mundaring. Complete the circuit by following Stoneville Rd south. Cross the highway and join up with the Kep Track to head back to the weir.

Photo: Mundaring Weir walkway
© Jo Hart

**74**

### Location
39km east from Perth

### Distance
15.7km circuit

### Grade
Medium

### Ideal Season
Winter

### Map
UBD 276 F11

### Notes
Dogs permitted
Multiple picnic spots
Signposted

Perth

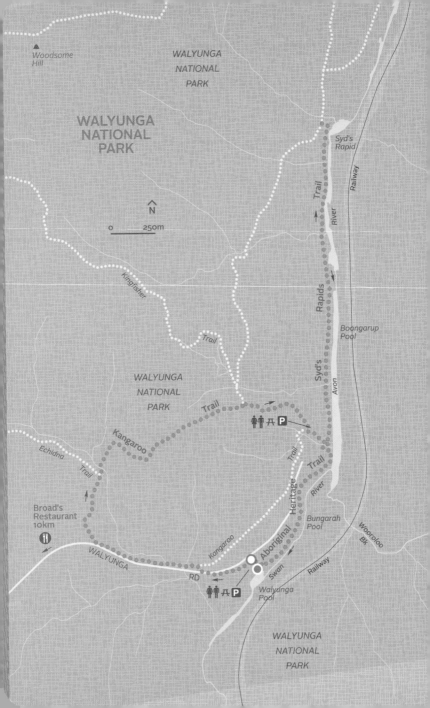

# SYD'S RAPIDS & ABORIGINAL HERITAGE TRAIL
## WALYUNGA NATIONAL PARK

75

Fascinating nature walk taking in the Avon Valley rapids. Walyunga has one of the largest-known Aboriginal campsites around Perth, where regional tribes met for more than 6000 years.

Start at Walyunga Pool, not far from where the Avon River turns into the Swan River, right in the heart of Walyunga National Park. Heavy winter rain transforms it into a wild ride for whitewater rafters; if you walk in drier months, it may be little more than puddles. Follow the 1.2km Aboriginal Heritage Trail in a clockwise direction towards Boongarup Pool. Interpretive signs reveal Aboriginal myths and legends, helping you to see the park's plants and animals through the original custodians' eyes. You'll finish up near a picnic area with facilities. From there, it's a flat, easy walk up to the rapids. Wander at your own pace along the riverbanks, observing the native bush, and listening for birds and rustling noises that indicate kangaroos. Eventually you'll reach Syd's Rapids. Return to your starting point. Refuel at Broad's Restaurant, Upper Reach Winery (77 Memorial Ave, Baskerville).

**Location**
40km north-east from Perth

**Distance**
6.4km circuit

**Grade**
Easy

**Ideal Season**
Winter

**Map**
UBD 153 N17

**Notes**
Aboriginal heritage
Park fees
Open daily from 8am-5pm

Photo: Walyunga Pool
© Elliot Keeney

Perth

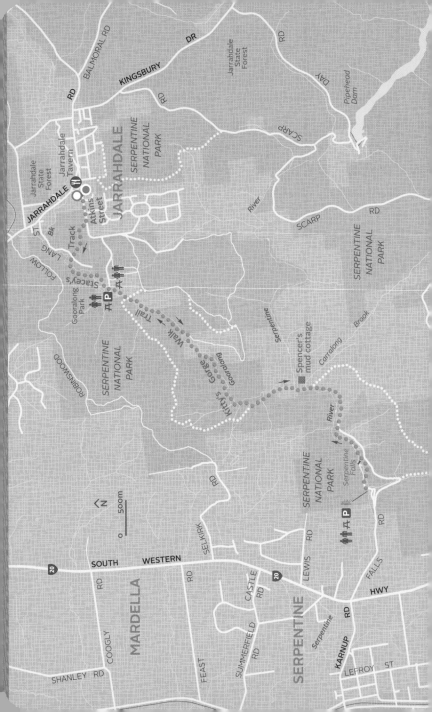

# KITTY'S GORGE
# WALK TRAIL
## SERPENTINE NATIONAL PARK

## 76

One of WA's most popular walks, Serpentine Falls is scenic and seductive. There are fantastic views of the Darling Range.

Quench your thirst at Jarrahdale Tavern (640 Jarrahdale Rd). Walk towards Atkins St and join Stacey's Track, which starts opposite the Jarrahdale Cemetery and brings you to Gooralong Brook. From here, Kitty's Gorge Walk Trail meanders through dense jarrah forest with large ferns near the water. While passing impressive granite outcrops and, after rain, a number of waterfalls, muse about the trail name – inspired by a cow named Kitty who wandered far from home and was found by the gorge months later. About halfway, beware the steep sections of rock with loose, uneven ground. Gooralong Brook gives way to the Serpentine River just before you come across Spencer's mud cottage. Not long after the two waterways converge, a steady climb leads to the stunning Serpentine Falls. There are picnic spots with barbeques. Be careful as you approach the falls. It can be slippery, and there have been fatalities. Always keep your eyes on the path. Return the way you came.

**Location**
60km south from Perth

**Distance**
14km return

**Grade**
Medium

**Ideal Season**
Winter

**Map**
UBD 483 L44

**Notes**
Steep sections
Uneven ground
Boardwalks
slippery when wet
Dangerous falls
Park entry fee

Photo: Serpentine Falls
© Chris Bartle

Perth

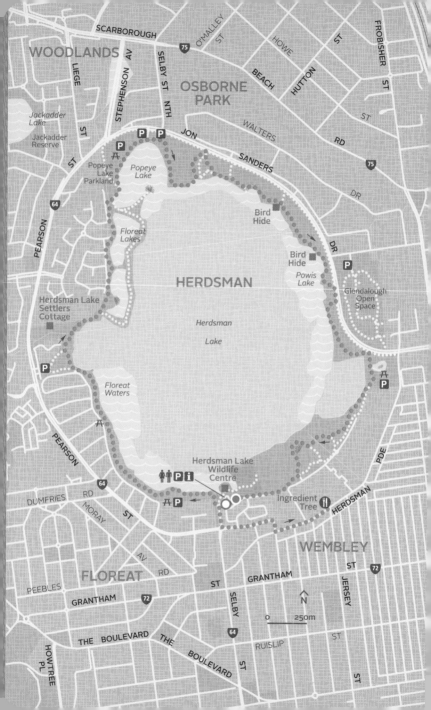

# HERDSMAN LOOP
## HERDSMAN LAKE REGIONAL PARK

Bulrushes, black swans, bird hides and walking trails surround this placid lake near the heart of the city, in 370ha of wetland and bush.

Start at the Herdsman Lake Wildlife Centre, viewing the lake from its top-floor bird observatory. Head west along a path through flooded gums and over a bridge. The path becomes limestone; continue with the lake on your right and after about 20 minutes, cross another bridge over Herdsman drain. There's a small track on the left, which is a nice detour to an old settlers cottage. Return to the main path and keep an eye out for rainbow bee-eaters nesting in tunnels in the bank on the left-hand side of the path. Northwards you'll hit Popeye Lake parkland where you can take one of the smaller, lakeside tracks to an observation site. There's a thick patch of flooded gums and two bird hides along the next stretch. Return to the wildlife centre and explore the numerous paths: walk through bulrush thickets and paperbark trees where night herons roost; watch for majestic black swans; and hear ducks and cormorants calling. Dine at the delectable Ingredient Tree cafe (87a Herdsman Pde, Wembley).

**77**

**Location**
6km north from Perth

**Distance**
8km circuit

**Grade**
Easy

**Ideal Season**
Spring

**Map**
UBD 267 D2

**Notes**
Dogs permitted Wildlife centre on site; gold-coin entry donation
Bird hides

Photo: Boardwalk through swamp paperbarks
© Ian Wallace

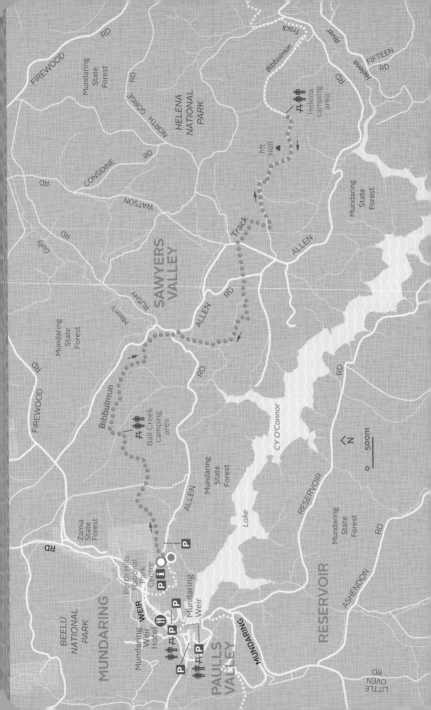

# BIBBULMUN TRACK,
## SECTION 1
### PERTH HILLS CENTRE TO HELENA CAMPSITE

## 78

Scenic taster of 1000km Bibbulmun Track walk, WA's longest, taking up to eight weeks to complete, and stretching from Perth to Albany.

Leaving the Perth Hills National Park Centre, follow the track through sheoak and jarrah forest – much of it is regrowth after felling years ago. The walk is even for about 2.5km as you approach Ball Creek camping area. About 1.5km beyond it, the track descends steeply then levels out along Mann's Gully. Be careful: the granite can become slippery when wet. From here, the terrain is more challenging, with a few steep, although short, ups and downs, and a climb through rocks and wandoo trees at about the 5.5km mark. Sublime views across the ridge make the effort worthwhile. The vista opens out at the 8km mark as you pass over exposed granite. Rest before tackling the final 3km to the campsite. Watch for the side trail on your right down to the Helena camping area. A steep descent brings you to a shelter, with spectacular views over the valley. Return the way you came, and enjoy a hearty meal at the nearby Mundaring Weir Hotel (Mundaring Weir Rd) with live music.

**Location**
39km east from Perth

**Distance**
22km return

**Grade**
Hard

**Ideal Season**
Spring

**Map**
UBD 276 K12

**Notes**
No dogs
Steep sections
Park centre open
Mon-Fri 10am-4pm

Photo: Between Helena and Ball Creek
© Laughing Ladies

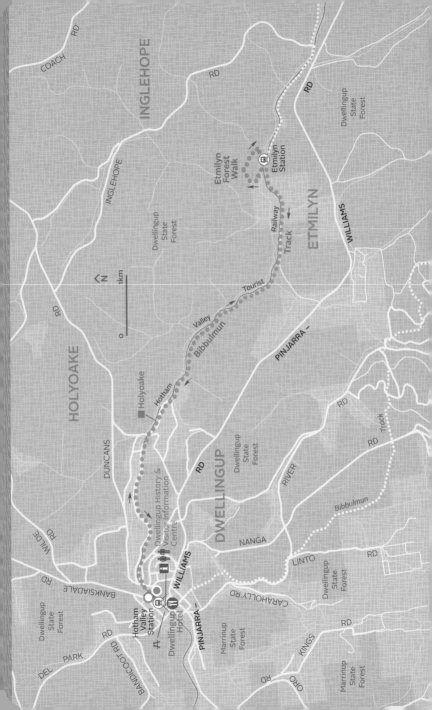

# BIBBULMUN TRACK,
## SECTION 2
### DWELLINGUP TO ETMILYN SIDING

Start with a historic timber-milling train trip before exploring towering WA jarrah forests. The historic locomotives, with open coaches and freight wagons, pass through stunning native forest. On board, you'll hear interesting commentary on WA's sawmilling and railway history.

Jump aboard the Dwellingup Forest Train at the Hotham Valley Tourist Railway, opposite the visitor centre. Alight at Etmilyn Siding, a place founded in the early 1920s as a watering point for steam locomotives. Have a look around and perhaps do the Etmilyn Forest Walk, a 1km loop through grass trees, banksias, blackbutts and red gums, which crosses over a number of little bridges. Walk clockwise before heading back along the Bibbulmun Track, which largely mirrors the train line, passing through jarrah forests and pine plantations. You'll pass signage commemorating the settlements that were lost in a catastrophic bushfire in 1961, including Holyoake, where there was once a large timber mill. Arrive at the Dwellingup Hotel (Marrinup St), an old timber-cutters haunt that's the only remaining community-owned hotel in WA.

79

**Location**
97km south from Perth

**Distance**
8.5km circuit

**Grade**
Easy

**Ideal Season**
Spring

**Notes**
No dogs
Train runs 10.30am and 2pm weekends, public and school holidays
Ticket sales cash only

Photo: Misty morning
© Pelusey Photography

Perth

# JOHN FORREST HERITAGE TRAIL
## JOHN FORREST NATIONAL PARK

80

Wilderness track through WA's first national park, alongside serene rockpools and impressive granite outcrops. Part of the 59km Railway Reserves Heritage Trail, this walk follows a railway line, built during the 1890s and closed in 1966.

Start the trail from the carpark at Pechey Rd, Swan View (cnr Morrison Rd). Walk through low scrub and watch out for blossoming wildflowers as the path edges towards a dirt track. At a Y-intersection, take the right-hand track and you'll soon pass through the 340m-long Swan View Tunnel, built to allow access through a granite barrier formed by a fold in the Darling Range. Take the left-hand track if you're claustrophobic. Further along, stop for a breather at National Park Falls. Continue to the three wooden trestle bridges, which are remnants of the old railway. Continue east to cascading Hovea Falls and relax in the picnic area with a bite to eat, or head to the Hovea Railway Platform and grab a drink at the Parkerville Tavern (6 Owen Rd), before returning the way you came.

**Location**
26km east from Perth

**Distance**
10.2km return

**Grade**
Medium

**Ideal Season**
Spring

**Map**
UBD 233 L14

**Notes**
Park fee $11
Waterfalls in spring and winter

Photo: Swan View Tunnel, John Forrest National Park
© Nicholas Woods

Perth

# BRISBANE
## QUEENSLAND

Nestled along the banks of the Brisbane River and fanning westward to the foothills of the Great Dividing Range and east to the Pacific Ocean, Brisbane is scribbled with walking tracks.

You can follow the waterway as it winds through the city, taking in stands of mangroves, soaring cliffs, city vistas and serene bushland humming to the tune of native birds, bats and brushtail possums. Ferries regularly ply the river so it's a cinch to leave your car at home and walk from one wharf to the next along well-worn paths and past historic Queenslander homes.

Venture further afield to explore the city's coastline where foreshore trails follow the sand and connect seaside hamlets. Enjoy some of the country's best seafood along the way.

Offshore, the Moreton Bay islands beckon. Walking is the best way to explore their sandy nooks and saltwater crannies: there's dunes to climb, lakes to plumb and crest-surfing dolphins, turtles, mantra rays and whales to spy.

To the city's north, the Glasshouse Mountains are impressive reminders of our land's volcanic past, and you can explore them on foot by following the walking tracks that skirt their base.

In the south, the Gold Coast hinterland conceals a treasure trove of natural wonders, from the ancient rainforests of Gondwana to cascading waterfalls and a stupefying collection of native wildlife.

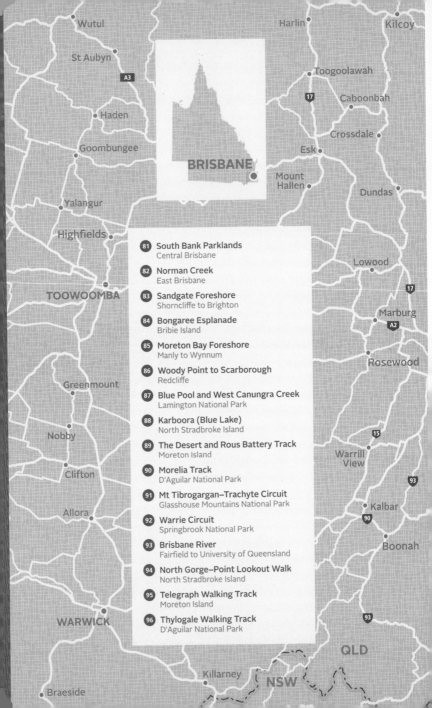

81 **South Bank Parklands**
Central Brisbane

82 **Norman Creek**
East Brisbane

83 **Sandgate Foreshore**
Shorncliffe to Brighton

84 **Bongaree Esplanade**
Bribie Island

85 **Moreton Bay Foreshore**
Manly to Wynnum

86 **Woody Point to Scarborough**
Redcliffe

87 **Blue Pool and West Canungra Creek**
Lamington National Park

88 **Karboora (Blue Lake)**
North Stradbroke Island

89 **The Desert and Rous Battery Track**
Moreton Island

90 **Morelia Track**
D'Aguilar National Park

91 **Mt Tibrogargan–Trachyte Circuit**
Glasshouse Mountains National Park

92 **Warrie Circuit**
Springbrook National Park

93 **Brisbane River**
Fairfield to University of Queensland

94 **North Gorge–Point Lookout Walk**
North Stradbroke Island

95 **Telegraph Walking Track**
Moreton Island

96 **Thylogale Walking Track**
D'Aguilar National Park

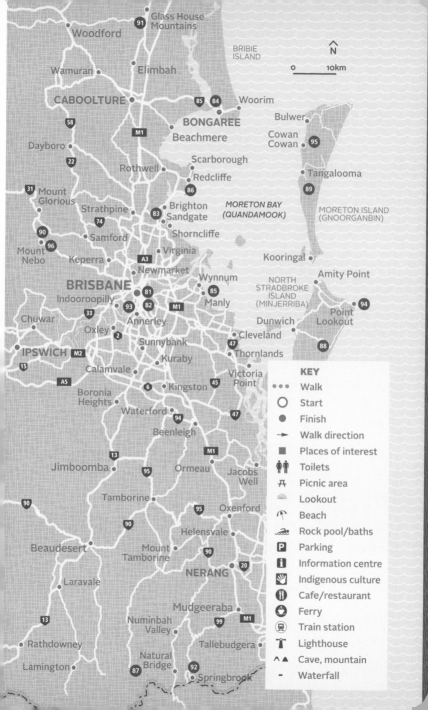

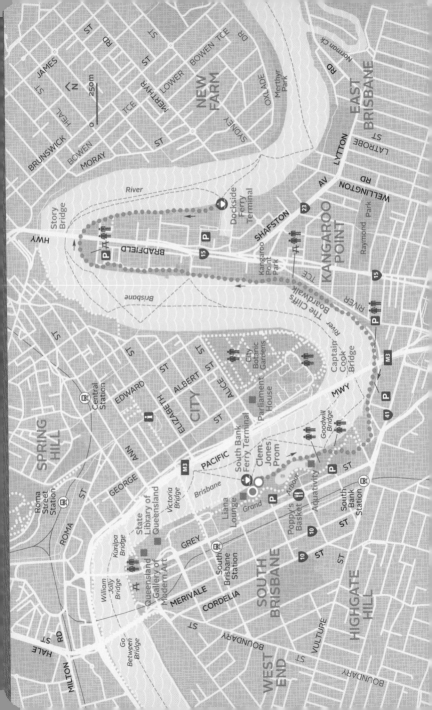

# SOUTH BANK PARKLANDS
## CENTRAL BRISBANE

Inner-city walk following the Brisbane River through South Bank Parklands and beneath dramatic, volcanic Kangaroo Point cliffs.

Fill your backpack with fresh fare at Poppy's Basket (Little Stanley St) before heading down to the South Bank Ferry Terminal 1. From here, meander along Clem Jones Promenade. Stop to cool off at Brisbane's inner-city beach or the interactive waterpark Aquativity before following the path to the Grand Arbour. Enjoy the shade of hot-pink bougainvillea en route to the Goodwill Bridge. After the entrance to the bridge, take the path to the river and trace the Cliffs Boardwalk to Captain Cook Bridge. You'll spy the rock wall of Kangaroo Point, formed from volcanic ash. Climb the steps to the top of the cliff for impressive river and city skyline vistas. Head back down and follow the river to the Story Bridge; at 777m, it's Australia's longest cantilever bridge. Once underneath it and around the point, you'll pass a parade of jacarandas to moor yourself at the Dockside Ferry Terminal. Return the way you came and enjoy a picnic beside the arbour or a little beyond your starting point at the Liana Lounge (next to the pagoda), a verdant spot with public art and the North Queensland liana vine.

**81**

**Location**
2km south-west from Brisbane

**Distance**
9km return

**Grade**
Easy

**Ideal Season**
Summer

**Map**
UBD 4 B14

**Notes**
Dogs permitted
Track sealed

Photo: South Bank Arbour
© Tourism Queensland, Barry Goodwin

Brisbane

# NORMAN CREEK
## EAST BRISBANE

This creekside wander skirts the banks of the Norman River through a bush corridor replete with twittering birds, mangroves, serene picnic spots and a colony of rowdy flying foxes.

Leave the car at home and catch the ferry to the Norman Park Ferry Terminal for the start of this East Brisbane walk. After you alight, take a minute in the ferry reserve to enjoy the river before heading up Wynnum Rd and Norman Ave before turning right into Scott St park. You'll find the start of the walkway here along with snatches of CBD views. At Griffin Park, follow the walkway and cross Bridgewater Creek before continuing downhill along the water. Look up and you'll see a 7000-strong resident colony of animated grey-headed flying foxes. Cross Stanley St and take the sealed path to the Common, then take the right-hand path to a walkway over Kingfisher Creek and follow the path to Langlands Park. From here, join Panitya St and have a dip at Langlands Park Memorial Pool or wander down to Lady Marmalade Cafe (cnr Logan Rd and Old Cleveland St) to refuel before heading back the way you came. Finish your walk at dusk and you'll likely see thousands of flying foxes taking off for their nightly foraging.

82

**Location**
6km east from Brisbane

**Distance**
9km return

**Grade**
Easy

**Ideal Season**
Summer

**Map**
UBD 24 B6

**Notes**
Dogs permitted
Track sealed
and unsealed

Photo: Grey-headed flying fox
© Mark Birchall

Brisbane

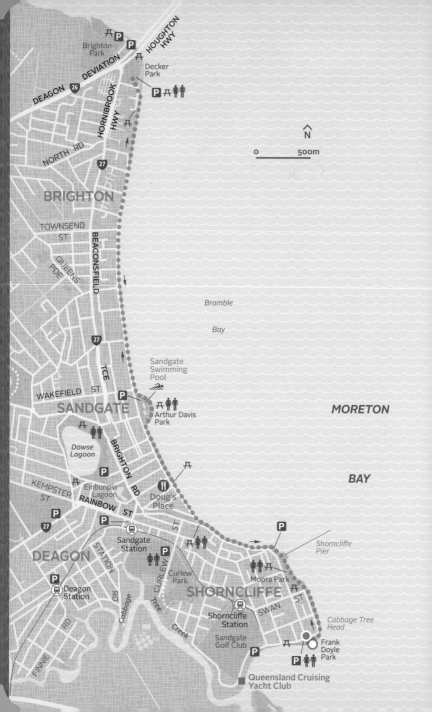

# SANDGATE FORESHORE
## SHORNCLIFFE TO BRIGHTON

Sea, sand and fish and chips at sunset define this enduring foreshore walk that revels in expansive Bramble and Moreton bay panoramas.

Enjoy the bobbing cruisers of the Queensland Cruising Yacht Club (moored in the mouth of Cabbage Tree Creek and to the right of your start point at Baxters Jetty carpark) before heading uphill to a lookout across the bay to Moreton Island. Continue along Shorncliffe Pde, hugging the shoreline as you pass Moora Park before reaching 350m-long Shorncliff Pier – you can't miss it, it has a sheltered pavilion about two-thirds of the way along. Back on the track, pass the Sandgate Swimming Pool. Unleash your inner child on the water slides, before pressing on, enjoying the sublime ocean vistas, watching pelicans sail on the wind, and listening to the soothing wash of waves on sand. Finish at Decker Park. In the distance you'll see three 2.7km-long bridges, which join Brisbane to seaside Redcliffe. If you're feeling energetic, use the dedicated pedestrian walkway to cross and continue along the path all the way to Redcliffe, or return the way you came, stopping for a bite at Doug's Place (60 Flinders Pde, Sandgate).

Photo: Shorncliffe Pier
© Chris Lofqvist

**83**

**Location**
21km north-east from Brisbane

**Distance**
7km one way

**Grade**
Easy

**Ideal Season**
Summer

**Map**
UBD 111 F9

**Notes**
Dogs permitted
Track sealed

Brisbane
———————

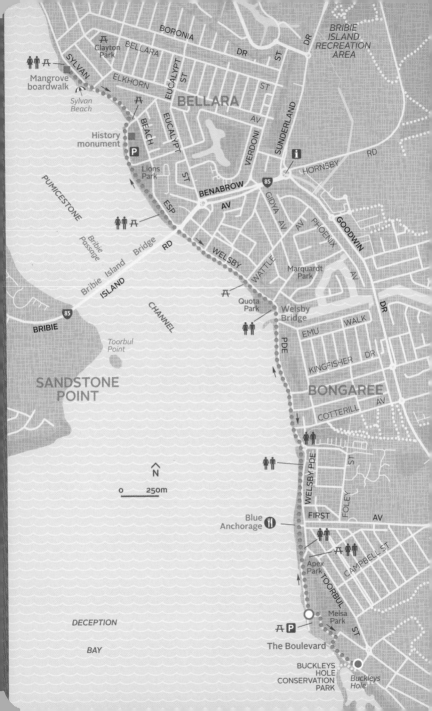

# BONGAREE ESPLANADE
## BRIBIE ISLAND

Foreshore track with enticing sandy beaches, pandanus palms, interesting wartime history and a fantastic bird hide.

Starting at the carpark at the southern end of South Espl, head north-west along the path, fringed by esplanade and sand, towards Bribie Island Bridge. Beyond this, it's an easy stroll along the sandy beach. Pass under Bribie Island Bridge and make your way to the silvery sliver of Sylvan Beach where there's a monument that tells of the area's WW II history, and beyond that is a timber path that wends through stilted mangroves. After this, the path enters private land – your cue to turn around and retrace your steps. Stop in at Blue Anchorage (2 Toorbul St). Lazing on the pandanus-fringed beachfront, it specialises in locally caught seafood. At walk's end, twitchers should continue south to the nature reserve Buckleys Hole, complete with freshwater lagoon and a bird hide. Nest here awhile and watch some of the 350-plus species of bird that inhabit the wetland and woods here.

84

**Location**
70km north-east
from Brisbane

**Distance**
7km return

**Grade**
Easy

**Ideal Season**
Summer

**Map**
UBD 63 D3

**Notes**
Dogs permitted
except at
Buckleys Hole
Track sealed

Photo: Comb-crested jacana mother and chick, Buckleys Hole
© Alan O'Leary

# MORETON BAY FORESHORE
## MANLY TO WYNNUM

85

With bookends of boat and beach, this lively foreshore track also has superb views of the sandy bubbles that are the Moreton Bay islands.

Take your time beginning this walk: sit silently and watch the bobbing pelicans and boats in Manly Harbour. From the parking area at the Wynnum Manly Yacht Club, trace the foreshore to Cambridge Pde and Manly Pool. Turn right into Wyvernleigh Cres and investigate William Gunn Jetty – stop for a coffee at the small cafe. Backtrack to Trafalgar St, turn right and follow the footpath to Norfolk Point; signage there highlights the smattering of islands in the bay. You can stop for lunch here at Wilson's Boathouse for delectable seafood, Tues–Sun. Head back the way you came and on to Eastwood Beach. Further along you'll pass Darling Point, Drevesen Park and heritage-listed Wynnum Wading Pool, opened in 1933. Finish your wander at Wynnum Jetty, decorated with local art and jutting into the briny beside Pandanus Beach. Refuel on freshly caught fish and tasty chips at Pelican's Nest by the Bay (143 The Esplanade) before returning to the start.

**Location**
20km east from Brisbane

**Distance**
9km return

**Grade**
Easy

**Ideal Season**
Autumn

**Map**
UBD 163 P6

**Notes**
Dogs permitted
Track sealed
Exposed

Photo: Wynnum sunrise
© Karl Hircock

Brisbane

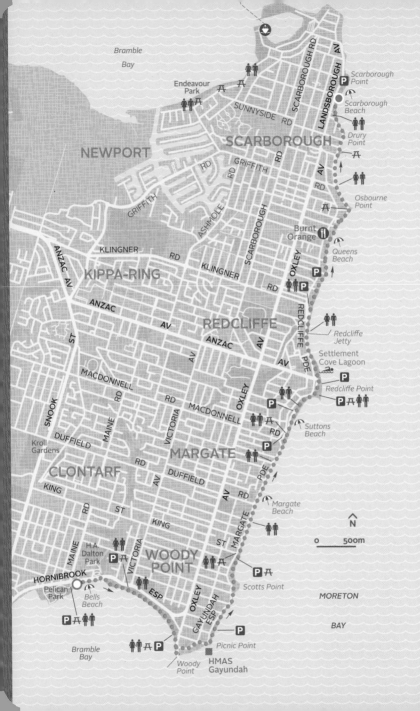

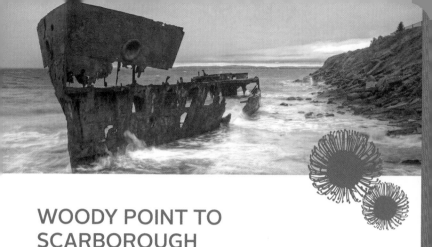

# WOODY POINT TO SCARBOROUGH

## REDCLIFFE

## 86

Coastal track along sheltered beaches with eye-popping ocean vistas and fascinating heritage sites.

From the breakwall alongside Pelican Park (off Hornibrook Espl), follow the path towards the boat ramp, and further on skirt the sandy stretch of Bells Beach. Regular onshore winds provide perfect conditions for kites; there is a kite-flying festival every May. At Woody Point, where Matthew Flinders stepped ashore in 1799, venture out along the 130-plus-year-old jetty before heading back the way you came, then turning right into Woodcliffe Cres and again into Lilla St. Rejoin the walking track and investigate the HMAS *Gayundah* shipwreck before following the footpath from Ellen St to Scotts Point Progress Park then head downhill to Margate Beach. At Suttons Beach, set your compass for Redcliffe Point. Wash away the day's heat in Settlement Cove Lagoon, a still, inviting pool, before reaching Redcliffe Jetty and beyond it Queens Beach and Drury Point. Finish your walk at Scarborough Beach Park and head to a favourite local haunt, Burnt Orange (95 Prince Edward Pde) for homemade everything.

**Location**
32km north-east
from Brisbane

**Distance**
11.5km one way

**Grade**
Medium

**Ideal Season**
Autumn

**Map**
UBD 91 F18

**Notes**
Dogs permitted
Track sealed
Exposed

Photo: HMAS *Gayundah* shipwreck
© Steve Dorman

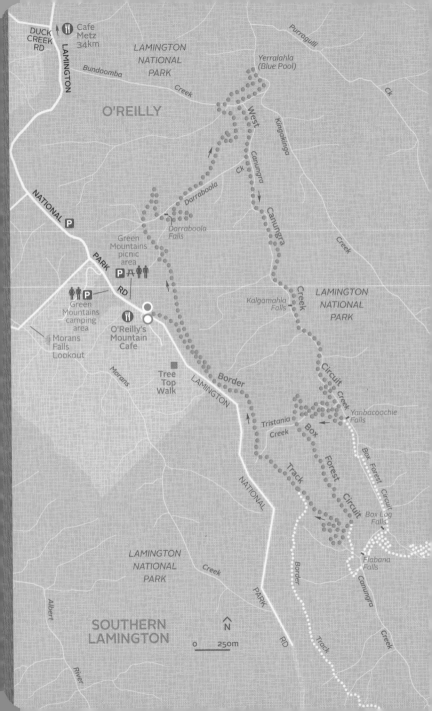

# BLUE POOL AND WEST CANUNGRA CREEK

## LAMINGTON NATIONAL PARK

Dramatic rainforest track with spectacular subtropical plants, long-drop waterfalls, elusive platypus and an inviting swimming hole.

Book an early lunch, complete with sublime rainforest views, on the expansive deck of O'Reilly's Mountain Cafe (Lamington National Park Rd), before following the signposted Border Track to its junction with Blue Pool Track. From here you descend steadily for around 400m. Revel in the subtropical rainforest – impressive stands of hoop pine, red cedar and booyong, with large staghorns– and mind the giant stinging trees and the leeches (pack some salt)! You will reach the pool: the perfect spot to cool off. Follow West Canungra Creek Circuit, splashing about in the water at marked creek crossings. Keep a look out for platypus and eels: beware the eels who bite when bothered. Passing Kalgamahla Falls, take the signposted Box Forest Circuit, stopping to watch the whitewater spray of Elabana Falls before rejoining the Border Track and return to the start. On your way home drop into laid-back Cafe Metz at Canungra (32 Christie St) to soak up the local vibe.

**Location**
85km south from Brisbane

**Distance**
13.9km circuit

**Grade**
Medium

**Ideal Season**
Autumn

**Notes**
No dogs
Track unsealed
Walk clockwise
Steep descent
Check track conditions with ranger before setting out

Brisbane

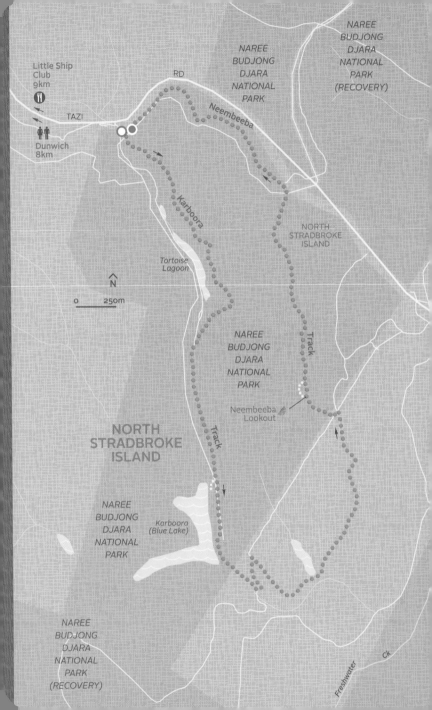

# KARBOORA (BLUE LAKE)
## NORTH STRADBROKE ISLAND

Soft sandy track through native wallum to a
peaceful blue pool, the ideal spot for a bush picnic.

**88**

Park on the side of Tazi (aka Trans Island) Rd and
pull on your walking shoes – the sun-scorched
sand will bake unprotected feet – before setting off
into Naree Budjong Djara National Park, created
to protect the island's freshwater lakes. The track
winds past Tortoise Lagoon, a small swamp on
your right. Further on, Karboora (which means
'deep, silent pool' in the local Quandamooka
language) is enveloped by bottlebrush, eucalypts
and paperbarks. It's a superb spot to while away
the hours, listening to native birdcalls and scanning
the bush for swamp wallabies and sand goannas.
While Karboora's gin-clear water is inviting, it's a
culturally significant place for the Quandamooka
people who ask that you don't swim there. Return
the way you came and, if you'd like to extend your
walk, tackle Neembeeba Lookout Walking Track
(6km return), which branches off to the left, for
panoramic views over the southern stretch of the
island, the Pacific Ocean and Gold Coast. Moor
yourself at the Little Ship Club for the freshest
seafood around (1 Yabby St, Dunwich).

**Location**
51km north-east
from Brisbane

**Distance**
10km return

**Grade**
Medium

**Ideal Season**
Autumn

**Map**
UBD 333 K20

**Notes**
No dogs
Track unsealed
Exposed
Includes ferry
ride from
Cleveland to
Dunwich

Photo: Karboora (Blue Lake), North Stradbroke Island
© Tourism Queensland, Peter Lik

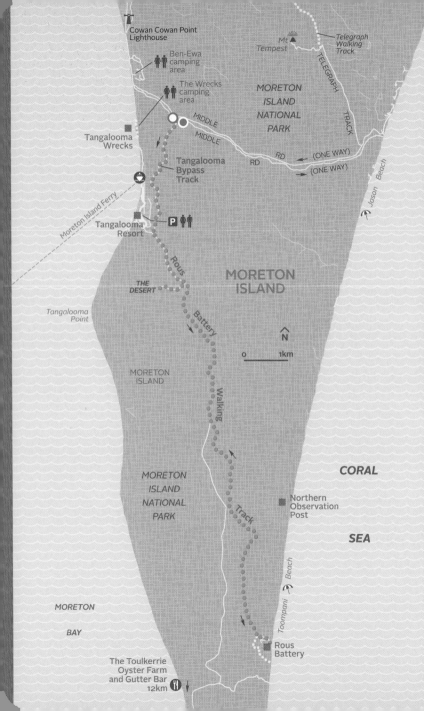

Cowan Cowan Point
Lighthouse

Ben-Ewa
camping
area

The Wrecks
camping
area

MIDDLE

MIDDLE

RD

Tangalooma
Wrecks

Tangalooma
Bypass
Track

Mt
Tempest

Telegraph
Walking
Track

TELEGRAPH

TRACK

MORETON
ISLAND
NATIONAL
PARK

RD (ONE WAY)

RD (ONE WAY)

Jason Beach

Moreton Island Ferry

P

Tangalooma
Resort

MORETON
ISLAND

Rous

THE
DESERT

Tangalooma
Point

Battery

N

0        1km

MORETON
ISLAND

Walking

MORETON
ISLAND
NATIONAL
PARK

Track

CORAL

Northern
Observation
Post

SEA

Toonpani Beach

MORETON

BAY

The Toulkerrie
Oyster Farm
and Gutter Bar
12km

Rous
Battery

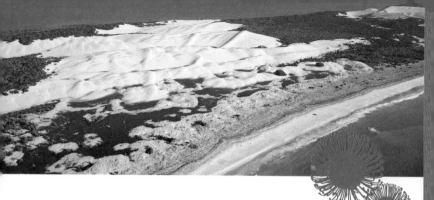

# THE DESERT AND ROUS BATTERY TRACK

## MORETON ISLAND

Snaking island track to historic WW II ruins with spectacular ocean vistas and a side trip to the gargantuan dunes of The Desert.

This walk on Moreton Island to Rous Battery follows a WW II supply road south-east across the sand. Park by the start of the signposted 4WD track on Middle Rd; the heat of the day falls away under a canopy of scribbly gums. The track skirts the resort area of Tangalooma, and about 3km from its start, breaks off to the right to The Desert – a massive dune system. Admire the view, then if you want to, slide to the bottom. Head back to the main track and continue south, passing through patches of feather-soft foxtail grass, especially beautiful backlit by the early morning or late afternoon sun. Take the left-veering track to the Northern Observation Post. The walls of the bunker are 30cm thick, designed to withstand shell mortars and stave off the beating island heat. Many of the ruins appear to have been swallowed by sand, but have, in fact, sunk. Explore the fort and watch for passing humpback whales and crest-surfing dolphins then return to the start. Call in at the Toulkerrie Oyster Farm and Gutter Bar (21 Kooringal Espl, Kooringal).

**Location**
65km north-east from Brisbane

**Distance**
13km one way

**Grade**
Medium

**Ideal Season**
Winter

**Notes**
No dogs
Track unsealed
Historic ruins
Bore water available;
treat before drinking

Brisbane

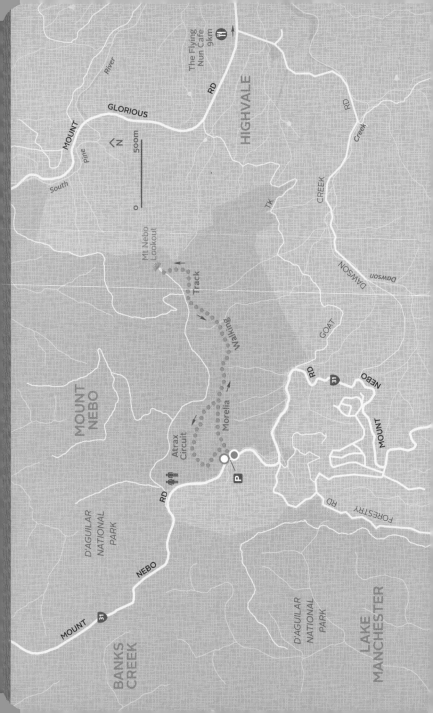

# MORELIA TRACK
## D'AGUILAR NATIONAL PARK

Enter an ancient forest on this well-defined track that delivers you to Mt Nebo Lookout with views of lush Samford Valley, Brisbane city and the azure water of Moreton Bay.

It's easy to get swept up in the grandeur of this walk: towering cabbage tree palms with large, fan-shaped leaves, strangler vines and mighty eucalypts provide a canopy of green. You'll also spot smaller wonders, like delicate frogs hopping through leaf litter and soft carpets of moss covering fallen logs. From the Manorina carpark on Mt Nebo Rd, follow the signs down the well-marked path into the rainforest. It's largely a gentle descent to Mt Nebo Lookout, although you'll be thankful for the vines and sturdy tree trunks that double as hand-holds in the steeper sections. Once you're there, stay and revel in the incredible scene laid out before you: the green valley, the urban sprawl and, finally, the inviting Pacific Ocean. Head back the way you came. For a detour, take a right at Atrax Circuit. Walk the circuit, rejoin the main track (turning right) and head back to the carpark. Refuel at the Flying Nun Cafe (16 Station St), located in a former Uniting church, complete with exquisite stained-glass windows, local art and Japanese tea pots.

90

**Location**
70km north-east from Brisbane

**Distance**
6km return

**Grade**
Medium

**Ideal Season**
Winter

**Notes**
No dogs
Track unsealed
Steep in parts

Brisbane

Photo: *Livistona australis* along the Morelia Track, D'Aguilar National Park
© Peter Richardson

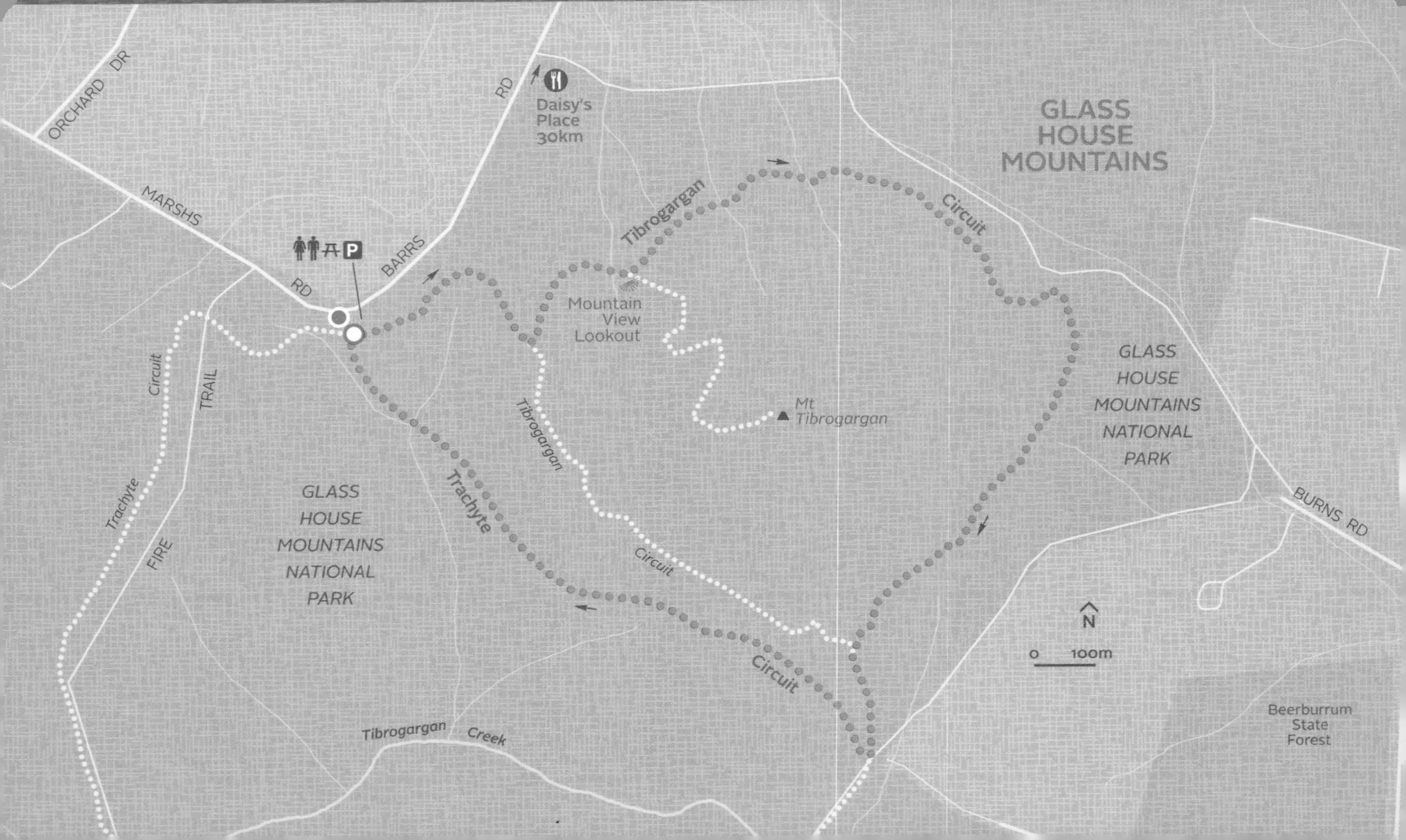

GLASS HOUSE MOUNTAINS

GLASS HOUSE MOUNTAINS NATIONAL PARK

Beerburrum State Forest

BURNS RD

N

0    100m

Circuit

Circuit

Circuit

Tibrogargan

Mt Tibrogargan

Mountain View Lookout

Tibrogargan

Trachyte

Daisy's Place 30km

RD

BARRS

RD

MARSHS

ORCHARD DR

GLASS HOUSE MOUNTAINS NATIONAL PARK

Tibrogargan Creek

Trachyte

FIRE

TRAIL

Circuit

# MT TIBROGARGAN–TRACHYTE CIRCUIT

## GLASSHOUSE MOUNTAINS NATIONAL PARK

## 91

This walk offers great views of Mt Tibrogargan, colloquially known as the Gorilla (from the east, it resembles a hunched ape). In the local Indigenous Gubbi Gubbi culture, Tibrogargan is a father figure: a fitting moniker for the most imposing peak in the Glasshouse Mountains.

Strike out from the northern end of the Mt Tibrogargan carpark and follow the Tibrogargan Circuit Track clockwise as it passes through casuarina groves, stands of gums and melaleuca forests. Continue on to Mountain View Lookout, where you can see some of the park's other 25 million-year-old volcanic remnants, such as Mt Beerwah and Mt Tunbubudla. From here you can access a pathway to the top of the 364m peak, but be warned, it's more a rock climb/scramble than a hike. Pick up the walking track around the base of Mt Tibrogargan, with interpretive signs providing details of the area's unique features. About two-thirds of the way around, join the Trachyte Circuit, which winds through state forest before returning you to your starting point on Barrs Rd. Make a beeline for the epicurean oasis Daisy's Place (2859 Steve Irwin Way, Glenview).

**Location**
66km north from Brisbane

**Distance**
9km circuit

**Grade**
Medium

**Ideal Season**
Winter

**Notes**
No dogs
Track unsealed
Exposed
Steep climb
to summit

Brisbane
―――――
205

Photo: Mt Tibrogargan
© David Anderson

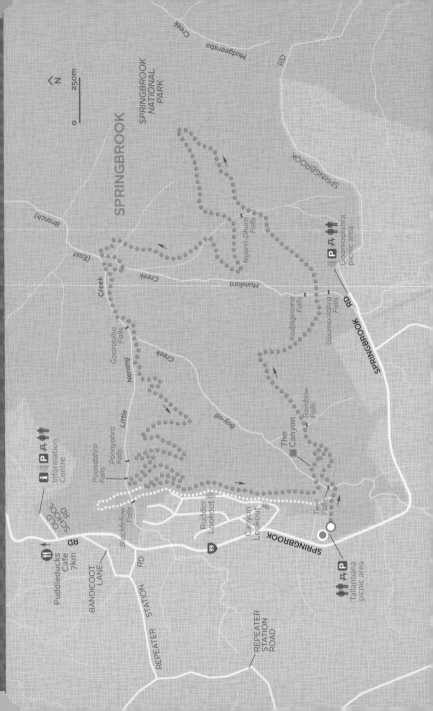

# WARRIE CIRCUIT
## SPRINGBROOK NATIONAL PARK

Lush rainforest circuit incorporating 11 waterfalls with a backdrop of sheer cliffs, making it one of the most spectacular walks in south-east Queensland.

**92**

This magnificent walk starts at Tallanbana picnic area and follows the base of the Canyon cliffs to Goomoolahra Falls. From here, the track, which can be slippery and hazardous in wet weather, crisscrosses a number of creeks (the track's name 'Warrie' is based on a local Indigenous word meaning 'rushing water') and gullies, and teems with life: look for crayfish in the water and the world's largest skinks warming themselves in the sun alongside the track. You might also hear lyrebirds calling from the forest. Continue along the well-worn path through a tangle of subtropical species including cabbage tree palms until you reach the base of the escarpment. As you climb you'll notice the vegetation change, from rainforest to towering eucalypts to scrubby heath. The climb out is steep and slow going; take your time and you'll be rewarded with sprawling views across the national park all the way to the skyscrapers of the Gold Coast. Reward your stomach with a hearty meal at Puddleducks Cafe (Springbrook Rd).

**Location**
100km south from Brisbane

**Distance**
17km circuit

**Grade**
Medium

**Ideal Season**
Winter

**Notes**
No dogs
Track unsealed
Walk anti-clockwise, leaving the short, sharp climb until the end
Creek crossings may be impassable after heavy rain

Brisbane

Photo: Warrie Circuit cascade
© Simon Baker

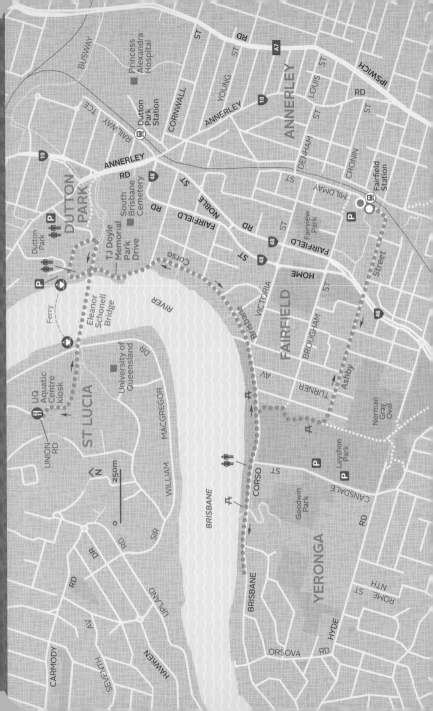

# BRISBANE RIVER
## FAIRFIELD TO UNIVERSITY OF QUEENSLAND

**93**

Riverside walk taking in blossoming natives, picturesque bushland, a meander across a nifty solar-powered bridge and a refreshing dip.

Using Fairfield Station as your base, walk along Mildmay and Ashby sts until you come to Leyshon Park. Join the Yeronga–Moorooka Bikeway; turn right and cross the Brisbane Corso to the riverside track. Turn left, enjoying the honeyeaters and red bottlebrush blooms as you walk. At track's end, turn around and follow the path back along the river. At the junction of Victoria and Newcastle sts, join the pathway along the Corso. Follow the track past South Brisbane Cemetery and along the river to pass under Eleanor Schonell Bridge. The green credentials of this bridge are impressive: solar power generates digital signs and lighting, and any runoff is cleaned then released into the river. Follow the path as it loops uphill, cross TJ Doyle Memorial Park Dr and take the right fork onto the 390m long, cable-strung span, then follow the path down to the river and continue on to the University of Queensland (UQ). Stop at the UQ Aquatic Centre kiosk (Union Rd) to refuel and soak up collegiate life before heading back the way you came.

**Location**
6km south from Brisbane

**Distance**
12km return

**Grade**
Easy

**Ideal Season**
Spring

**Map**
UBD 179 Q9

**Notes**
Dogs permitted
Track sealed
Beware cyclists on blind corners
Starts and finishes at railway station

Photo: Bottlebrush
© Rosie Nicolai

Brisbane

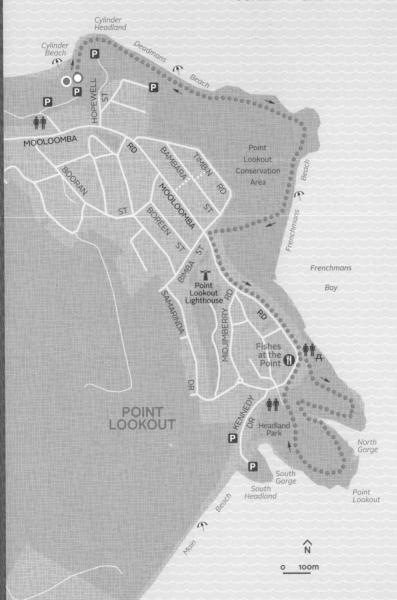

CORAL SEA

Cylinder
Headland

Deadmans

Beach

Cylinder
Beach

MOOLOOMBA

Point
Lookout
Conservation
Area

HOPEWELL ST

BOORAN

RD

BAMBARA

TIMBIN RD

MOOLOOMBA

ST

BOREEN

ST

BIMBA ST

SAMARINDA

DR

Frenchmans Beach

Frenchmans
Bay

Point
Lookout
Lighthouse

MIDJIMBERRY RD

RD

Fishes
at the
Point

KENNEDY DR

POINT
LOOKOUT

Headland
Park

North
Gorge

South
Gorge

South
Headland

Main Beach

Point
Lookout

N

0    100m

# NORTH GORGE–POINT LOOKOUT WALK

## NORTH STRADBROKE ISLAND

94

Magnificent walk exploring sandy beaches and craggy headlands with whale- and dolphin-watching par for the course.

Coastal walks rarely serve up better than this. From the Cylinder Beach carpark (off Mooloomba Rd), walk through the banksias to the Pacific Ocean. Keeping the whitewash to your left, head east to the headland at the end of the sand. Climb the rocks: use binoculars to spot sea turtles and manta rays. At the western end of Deadmans Beach, explore the rockpools. Walk along then round a cliff to arrive at beautiful (unpatrolled) Frenchmans Beach. Near its end, take the timber steps through a snag of banksias, pandanus and she-oak to the summit. Turn left and take the path along Mooloomba Rd to a grassy knoll, ideal for whale spotting between June and November, and the start of the North Gorge Walk. Continue along the track and climb to the top of a hill; nearby is a blowhole (don't venture too close). Then head to a lookout over South Gorge. Follow the track, then return to Cylinder Beach. To sample the local piscatorial fare, visit Fishes at the Point (15 East Coast Rd).

**Location**
60km north-east from Brisbane

**Distance**
6km return

**Grade**
Medium

**Ideal Season**
Spring

**Map**
UBD 334 L16

**Notes**
Dogs permitted
Track unsealed
Exposed
Avoid at high tide

Brisbane

Photo: North Gorge
© Tourism Queensland, Barry Goodwin

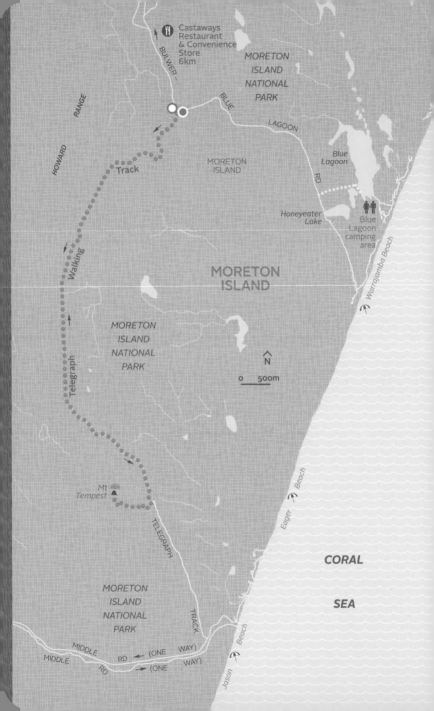

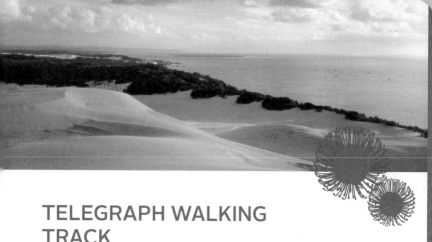

# TELEGRAPH WALKING TRACK

## MORETON ISLAND

95

Wild island track to the summit of the world's highest sand dune, providing views across Moreton Bay Marine Park to the Gold and Sunshine coasts and west to the Glasshouse Mountains.

Stay overnight at Blue Lagoon camping area and rise early to tackle this untamed walk off Bulwer–Blue Lagoon Rd. Leave your car at the start of the track and follow it through coastal heath and scribbly gums until, after approximately 60 minutes, you reach a swamp on your right. Look for remnants of the now defunct telegraph line, constructed in the late 1800s to connect Queensland's first lighthouse at rocky Cape Moreton with fellow Moreton Bay islands. Look also for the profusion of hardy spring wildflowers. At walk's end, challenge yourself by climbing to the 280m crest of Mt Tempest, the island's highest point. There's a seat at the summit so you can stay awhile and savour the all-encompassing views. Look for humpbacks and dugongs. Head back the way you came and swim in the fresh water of Blue Lagoon, which is surrounded by tea trees. Make tracks to Castaways Restaurant & Convenience Store (100 Moreton St, Bulwer).

**Location**
75km north-east from Brisbane

**Distance**
16km return

**Grade**
Medium

**Ideal Season**
Spring

**Notes**
No dogs
Track unsealed
4WD required to reach start of walk

Brisbane

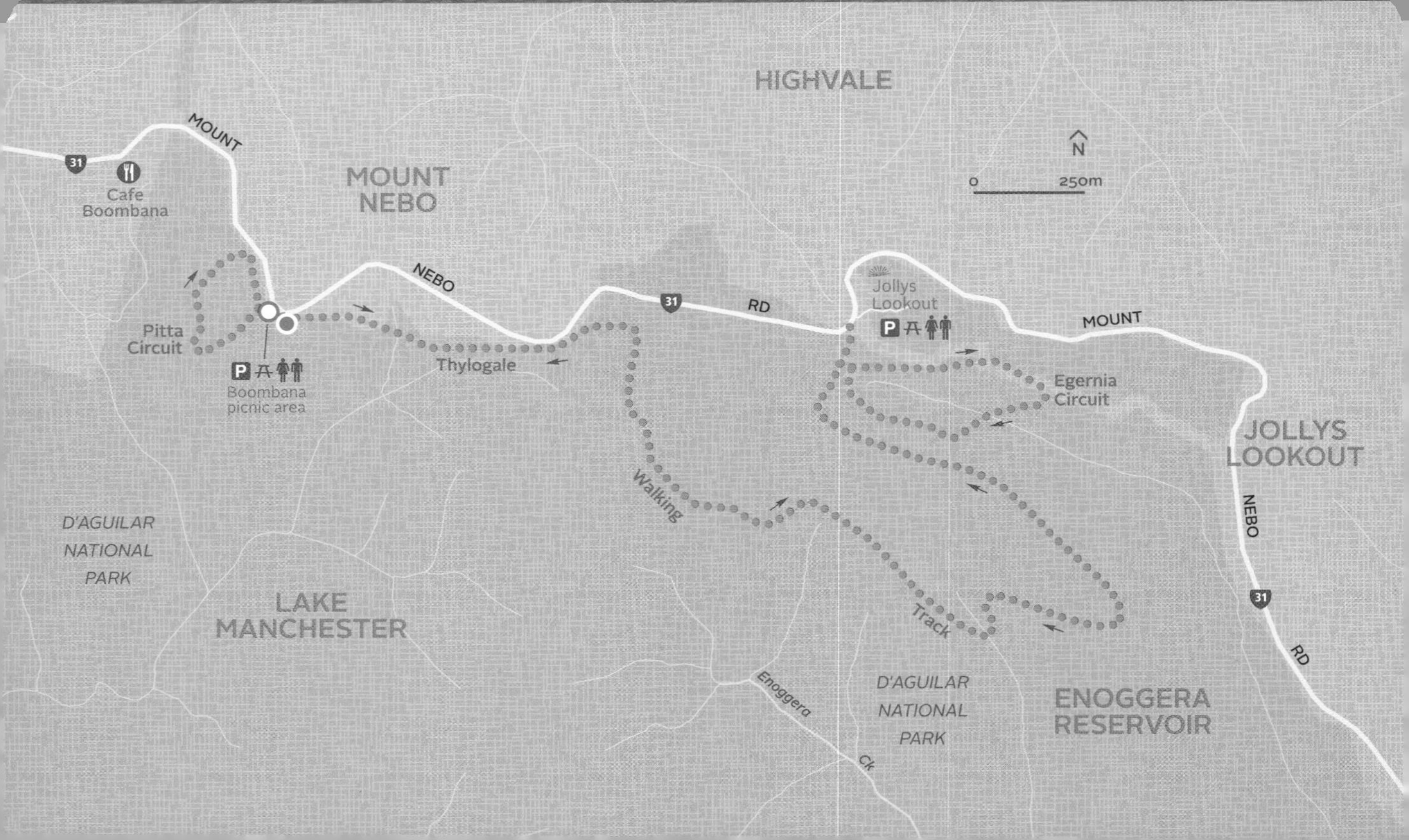
HIGHVALE
MOUNT NEBO
Cafe Boombana
31
MOUNT
NEBO
RD
MOUNT
NEBO
RD
N
0
250m
Pitta Circuit
Boombana picnic area
Thylogale
Walking
Track
Jollys Lookout
Egernia Circuit
JOLLYS LOOKOUT
D'AGUILAR NATIONAL PARK
LAKE MANCHESTER
Enoggera
Ck
D'AGUILAR NATIONAL PARK
ENOGGERA RESERVOIR

# THYLOGALE WALKING TRACK
## D'AGUILAR NATIONAL PARK

## 96

Remote bush track through stands of eucalypts and subtropical rainforest to Jollys Lookout with a side trip to view a behemoth strangler fig.

Boost your energy levels with brunch, or pick up lunch-to-go, at Cafe Boombana (1863 Mt Nebo Rd, Mt Nebo) before making your way to Boombana picnic area for the start of this circuit track, which drips with native wisteria flowers in the spring. Take your time as you wend through the scribbly gums and go quietly: you might just spot wompoo fruit-doves, yellow-tailed black-cockatoos and bowerbirds stashing their wares in ground nests along the way. You'll need to visit at night to spy the nocturnal masters of the forest: short-eared possums, yellow-bellied gliders and the powerful owl, which is listed as vulnerable. At the halfway point, enjoy the views from Jollys Lookout – hundreds of hectares of bush laid out before you like a woolly green carpet. Return the way you came or tackle peaceful Egernia Circuit before heading back to the picnic area and onto the 1.1km Pitta Circuit, worth the effort for the impressive strangler fig en route. Enjoy your takeaway fare before bidding the park adieu.

**Location**
73km north-west from Brisbane

**Distance**
8km return

**Grade**
Medium

**Ideal Season**
Spring

**Notes**
No dogs
Track unsealed

Photo: Small-leaved fig
© Neil Gavin

Brisbane

# HOBART
## TASMANIA

Australia's southernmost city is a walker's Eden with the heating turned down a touch. Explore the historic places and spaces of the country's second oldest capital by following the courses of its urban rivulets to extraordinary buildings in unexpected locations; or by seeking out the gates of a long-gone zoo before wandering the lush reaches of nearby Royal Tasmanian Botanical Gardens.

Embrace Hobart's positioning on the River Derwent by strolling the foreshores to a charming string of boatsheds or walking the eastern shore for views back across to the city and Mt Wellington.

Out of town you'll find old tramway routes, the ghosts of a forgotten mining settlement, pockets of rainforest, a hidden waterfall and an exposed surfing beach to wander and comb.

Venture even further from the city to see the autumn colours of the fagus reflected in alpine lakes, the spring wildflowers of the southwest and vertiginously high dolerite sea cliffs plunging into the Tasman Sea. Take a ferry to Bruny Island and imagine, while you hike, how much easier it might be to pronounce Labillardiere Peninsula if the French had decided to colonise Tasmania. When the days are long and there's no snow forecast, trek to the rocky summit of Hartz Peak.

Whatever you choose to do in whichever season, rest assured that hot chocolate is sold just about everywhere.

Photo: Snowgums, Tasmania © Rob Blakers, Getty Images
Photo: Freshly picked cherries © Pumpkins, Shutterstock.com

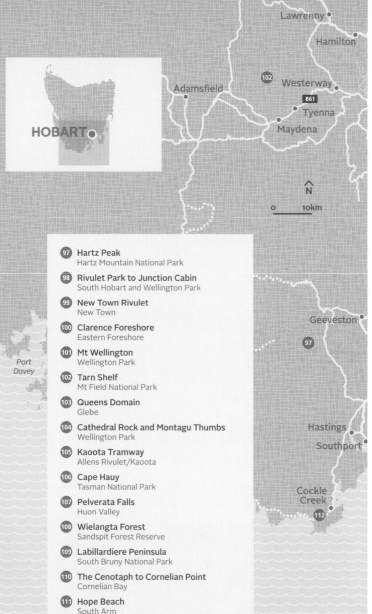

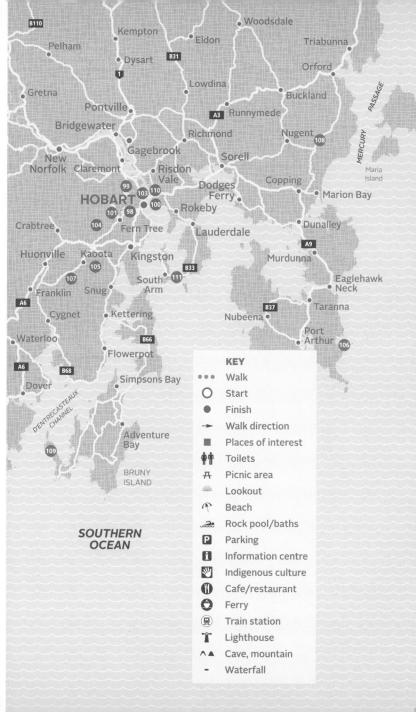

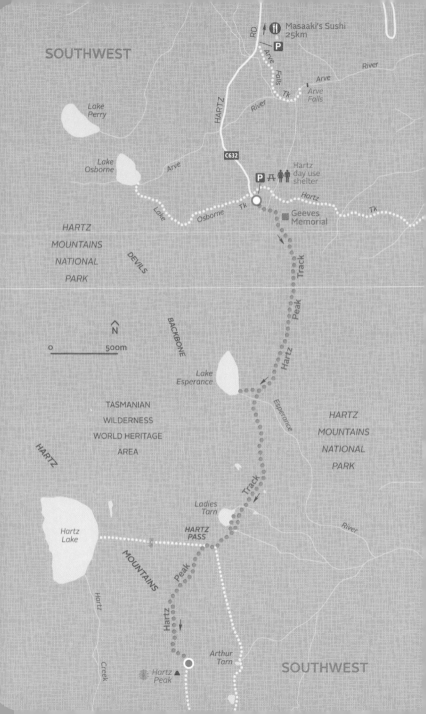

# HARTZ PEAK
## HARTZ MOUNTAIN NATIONAL PARK

97

Gorgeous walk through subalpine moorland and across splintered dolerite scree to the highest point in this World Heritage national park. Hartz Peak was one of the state's earliest popular bushwalking destinations. Be prepared for extreme weather changes (blizzard conditions can occur in summer).

From the Parks and Wildlife shelter, follow the well-marked track to a small tract of alpine bushland. Emerge from the trees into a landscape of exposed subalpine moor and heathland with Hartz Peak in clear view up ahead – when the view is clear. Divert to Lake Esperance and Ladies Tarn to see cushion plants and even a platypus in one of these glacial lakes. Listen out for the moss froglet, which sounds like a bouncing ping-pong ball. About halfway to Hartz Peak, the track splits. Head left and cross a scree slope marked with exquisitely designed cairns. From the weathered dolerite columns of the summit, resembling an ancient city, the view will either be into the Southwest National Park or a cloud. On the way back to Hobart, drop into Masaaki's Sushi (20b Church St, Geeveston) for superb Japanese food.

**Location**
84km south-west
from Hobart

**Distance**
9km return

**Grade**
Medium

**Ideal Season**
Summer

**Notes**
No dogs
Track sealed
and unsealed

Hobart

Photo: View of Hartz Peak
© Roger Wong

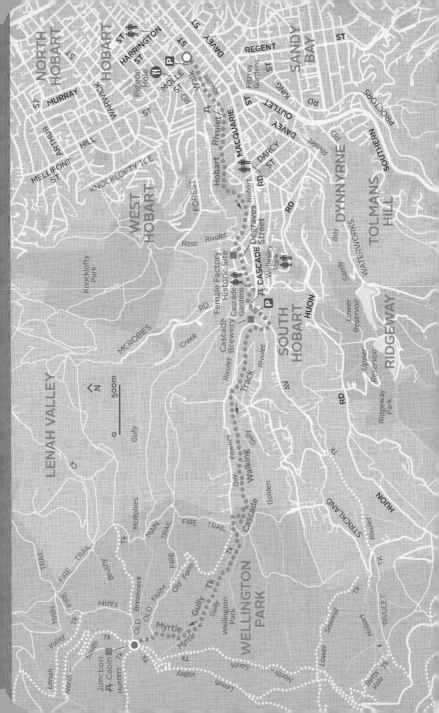

# RIVULET PARK TO JUNCTION CABIN

## SOUTH HOBART AND WELLINGTON PARK

## 98

Picturesque walk following the watercourse from the edge of the city centre into the foothills of Mt Wellington.

Start the day in Hobart's much-loved Pigeon Hole cafe (93 Goulburn St), and, before you leave, add a crostata to your picnic lunch. The track begins nearby at the lowest point of Molle St where the Hobart Rivulet disappears under the city. For centuries this was a source of drinking water for the Mouheneener band of the South-East people; then later the pristine creek provided an ideal environment for a convict settlement. Walk alongside the willow-lined waters towards its catchment area of Mt Wellington. The striking facade of the historic Cascade Brewery marks the end of the Rivulet Park and the beginning of the Cascade Walking Track. From behind the brewery, follow markers up to where the rivulet flows through a green mossy gully flanked by rainforest. The adjoining Myrtle Gully Track is even steeper and even greener. If the sight and setting of Junction Cabin are not reward enough, remember it's downhill all the way back.

**Location**
1.5km south-west from Hobart

**Distance**
15km return

**Grade**
Medium

**Ideal Season**
Summer

**Notes**
Dogs permitted
Track unsealed
Creek crossings may be impassable after heavy rainfall

Photo: Junction Cabin
© Steve Bromley

Hobart

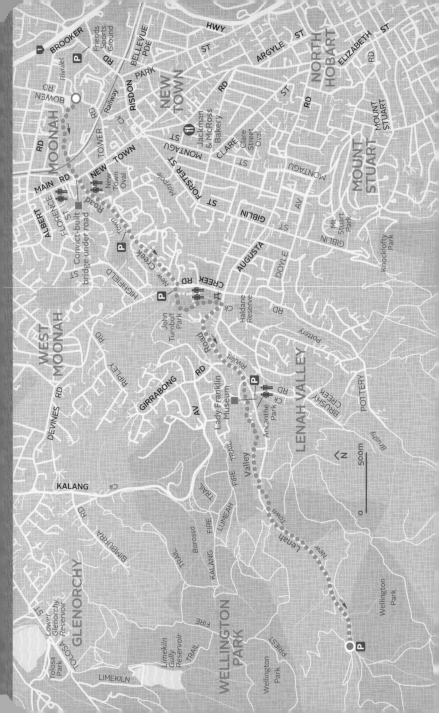

# NEW TOWN RIVULET
## NEW TOWN

Creekside walk from suburban New Town into natural bushland taking in a historic bridge, museum and houses along the way.

99

Take a seat at Jackman & McRoss Bakery in New Town (32 Cross St) to fill up and gather supplies for later. Start walking from the bridge on Bowen Rd opposite Wilmslow Ave. From there it's a gentle rise all the way from sea level to just over 250m. New Town was where the first governor of Hobart allowed free settlers to build their homes – well away from the convict settlement – and they did so on either side of the local water supply. This higgledy-piggledy track leads you through an urban environment and up into bushy foothills where the rivulet cascades through sandstone and all tracks lead to Mt Wellington. Look for the convict-built bridge at the intersection of Creek Rd and New Town Rd. Later you'll pass Lady Franklin Museum, which was constructed in 1842 in the style of a Grecian temple and is fantastically incongruous with its surroundings. Built in the hope of igniting the colony's interest in culture and the arts, the building was used, amongst other things, to store apples. When you reach the end, break out the pastries and enjoy a bush picnic.

**Location**
5.5km north from Hobart

**Distance**
15km return

**Grade**
Medium

**Ideal Season**
Summer

**Notes**
Dogs allowed
Track sealed and unsealed

Photo: New Town Rivulet
© Andrew Fuller

Hobart

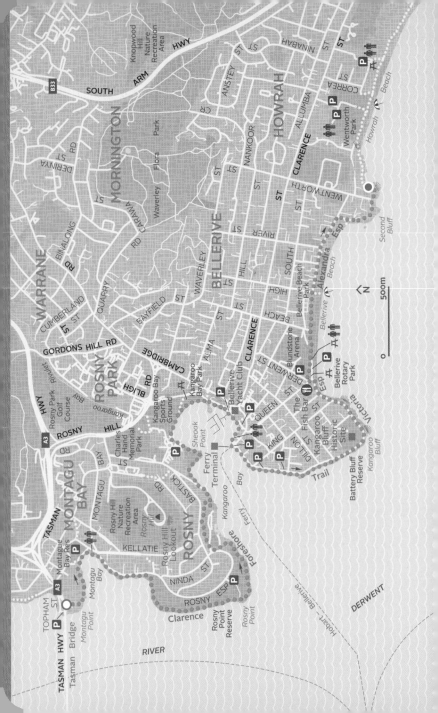

# CLARENCE FORESHORE
## EASTERN SHORE

Relaxing walk along the eastern foreshore with views of Hobart and out to the mouth of the River Derwent. This side of the River Derwent catches the afternoon sun, even in winter, which is why Hobart locals call it 'the sunny eastern shore'.

Follow the gravel road off Topham St to locate the parking spot under the Tasman Bridge where the Clarence Foreshore Trail is signposted. This foreshore trail follows the natural curve of the shoreline around Rosny, Bellerive (pronounced bell-reev) and Howrah. Mt Wellington, across the water, is almost always in sight and the views out to South Arm and the mouth of the river are sublime. The Fish Bar (51 Queen St, Bellerive) is the perfect lunch spot whatever the weather. Have takeaway on Bellerive Beach or pick a selection of seasonal seafood, grab a booth and soak in the local atmosphere. The lookout over Howrah Beach – a sculpted bench under a single pine tree – is a good place to turn around and head home. Drop back into the Fish Bar for delicious Tasmanian-made ice cream.

**100**

Location
5km north-east
from Hobart

Distance
18km

Grade
Medium

Ideal Season
Summer

Notes
Dogs permitted
Track mainly
sealed

Hobart

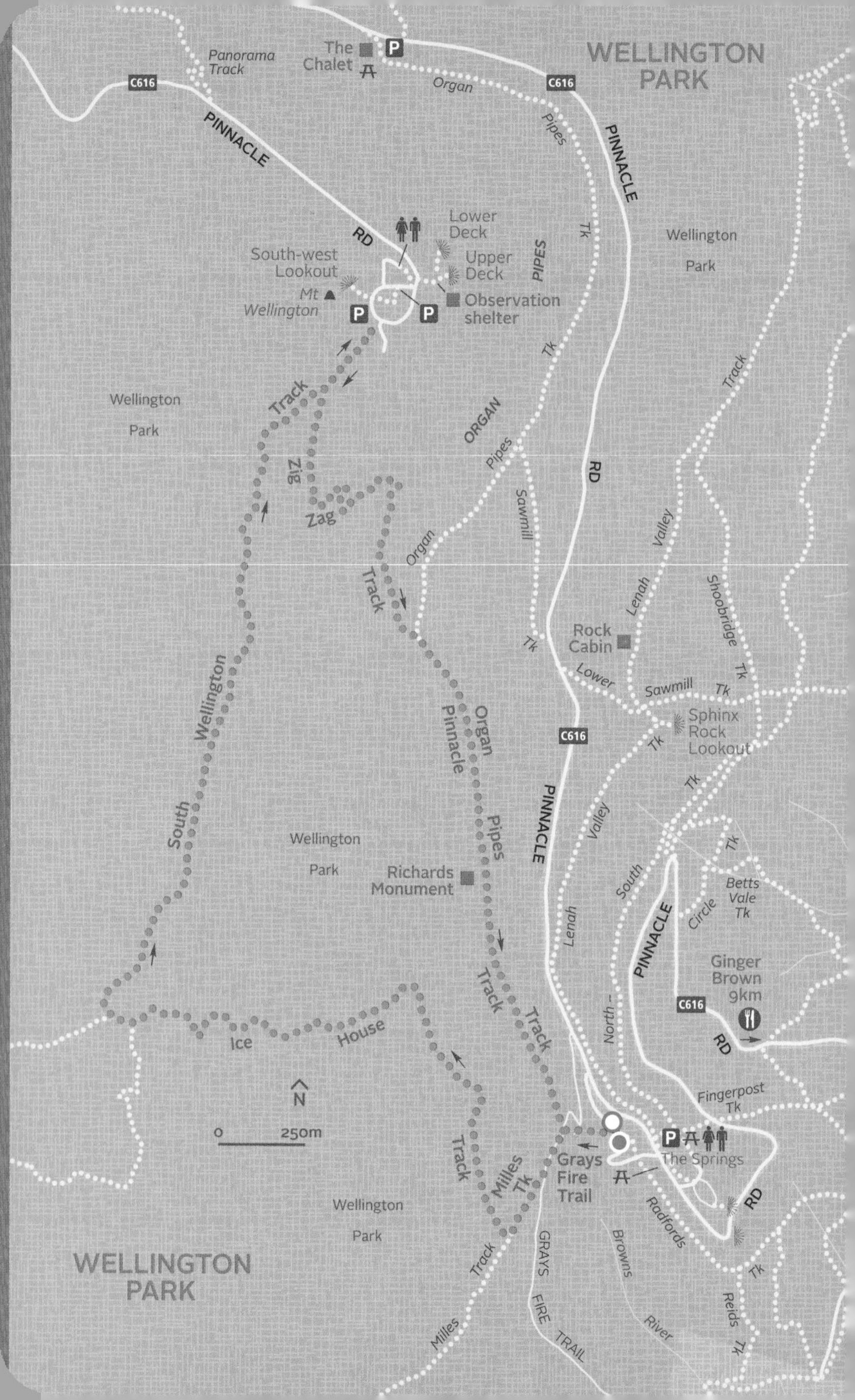
WELLINGTON PARK
Panorama Track
The Chalet
C616
Organ
Pipes
PINNACLE
RD
PINNACLE
Tk
Lower Deck
Upper Deck
South-west Lookout
Mt Wellington
Observation shelter
PIPES
Wellington Park
Wellington Park
Track
Zig
Zag
ORGAN
Pipes
Tk
Track
Organ
Sawmill
RD
Valley
Lenah
Shoobridge
Tk
Track
Rock Cabin
Tk
Lower
Sawmill
Tk
Sphinx Rock Lookout
C616
Tk
Tk
Organ
Pinnacle
South
Wellington
Pipes
PINNACLE
Valley
Wellington Park
Richards Monument
Tk
South
Betts Vale Tk
Circle
Lenah
PINNACLE
Ginger Brown 9km
C616
Track
Track
North -
RD
Ice
House
N
0 250m
Fingerpost Tk
The Springs
Track
Milles Tk
Grays Fire Trail
RD
Radfords
Wellington Park
Browns
WELLINGTON PARK
Track
GRAYS
FIRE
TRAIL
Milles
River
Tk
Reids
Tk

# MT WELLINGTON
## WELLINGTON PARK

Steep loop past historic ruins, across the rocky alpine plateau and down the dolerite face of the mountain. Along the way, keep an eye out for the rubbly ruins of three buildings that provided ice to Hobart before the days of fridges and freezers. These structures were packed with ice and snow then heavily insulated with straw or sawdust so that ice was available throughout summer. Be prepared for extreme weather changes (snow can occur in summer).

Before conquering Mt Wellington, fill up with a hearty breakfast at Ginger Brown (464 Macquarie St, South Hobart). The cafe sources organic and free-range products, bakes gluten-free bread and doesn't skimp on the bacon. Park at the Springs and follow Grays Fire Trail then Milles Track to locate Ice House Track. This rocky path will lead you up more than half a kilometre in altitude into alpine forest and heathland. Follow South Wellington Track to the summit, negotiating boulders and watercourses along the way, before enjoying the superb sweeping views or the mesmerising mist at the top of this mountain. Return via the Zig Zag Track, which takes you down the face, then join Organ Pipes Track back to the Springs.

**101**

**Location**
13km south-west
from Hobart

**Distance**
8.2km circuit

**Grade**
Hard

**Ideal Season**
Autumn

**Notes**
No dogs
Track unsealed

Hobart

Photo: View of Hobart from Mt Wellington
© Tourism Tasmania, Garry Moore

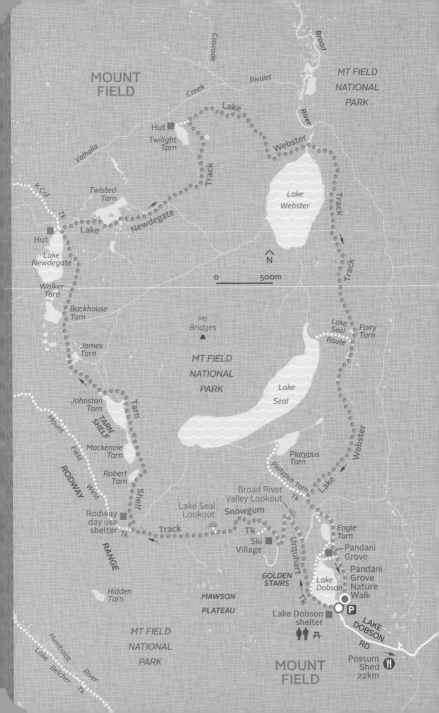

# TARN SHELF
## MT FIELD NATIONAL PARK

Moderately challenging circuit through undulating alpine landscape of tarns, lakes, dolerite boulders and historic huts. Be prepared for extreme weather changes (blizzard conditions can occur in summer).

Make an early start for a long day of walking and gawking through the glacially formed alpine section of this national park. Start from the carpark at Lake Dobson. Walk the lake's western shore through groves of exotic-looking pandani palm and up past the ski club buildings to where the track really begins. In late April, the deciduous fagus are at their multi-coloured height, with their leaves reflecting in the glacial tarns spaced along the ice-scoured ledge of Tarn Shelf. You'll pass huts along the way in which to shelter if the weather, like the fagus, has turned. As you negotiate the circuit's boardwalks and rocky paths, try to imagine this landscape in winter, when the tarns and lakes freeze and snow covers the buttongrass plains and alpine heath. For the final kilometre back to the carpark, the track becomes a pandani-lined road. If you have time, look for platypus in Lake Dobson, though the riverside Possum Shed (1654 Gordon River Rd, Westerway) does offer resident platypus-spotting with afternoon tea.

**102**

**Location**
89km north-west
from Hobart

**Distance**
13km circuit

**Grade**
Medium

**Ideal Season**
Autumn

**Notes**
No dogs
Track unsealed
and can be
very rocky
Only walk if
weather is fine

Hobart

Photo: Tarn shelf
© Nathan Deutschbein

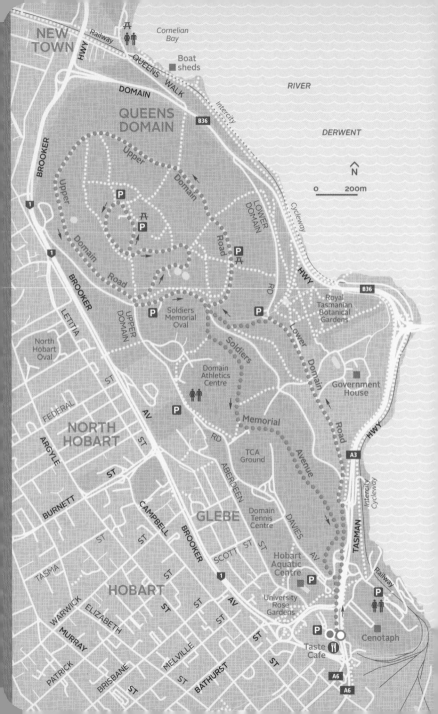

# QUEENS DOMAIN
## GLEBE

Interesting circuit through the city's historic domain passing the old zoo, entrance to the botanical gardens and memorial to local soldiers.

Begin with muffins and chai at Taste Cafe in the Baha'i Centre for Learning (1 Tasman Hwy) and walk from there. Before long the sound of the Tasman Hwy is replaced by native birdcalls – eastern rosella, yellow wattle bird, cockatoo. Wind through the oak trees as you venture deeper into Queens Domain. Aboriginal middens have been found here and, since colonial times, it's been the site for many things, including anti-conscription rallies and a tent city for the homeless after World War I. You'll soon pass the gates of Beaumaris Zoo that is now, like the last thylacine pacing its cage here until 1936, just a memory. Further along, detour into the lush and otherworldly confines of the botanical gardens before cutting between roads on the Grassland Gully track, which takes you through rare native grassland. Follow the concentric circuits up to the highest point in the domain and return to walk between the cedar and cypress trees, planted in 1918, of Soldiers Memorial Ave. By now you're on the home stretch.

**103**

**Location**
Central Hobart

**Distance**
7km circuit

**Grade**
Medium

**Ideal Season**
Autumn

**Notes**
Dogs permitted
Track sealed
and unsealed

Photo: Commemorative arch, Botanical Gardens
© CC Jeaneeem

Hobart
———
233

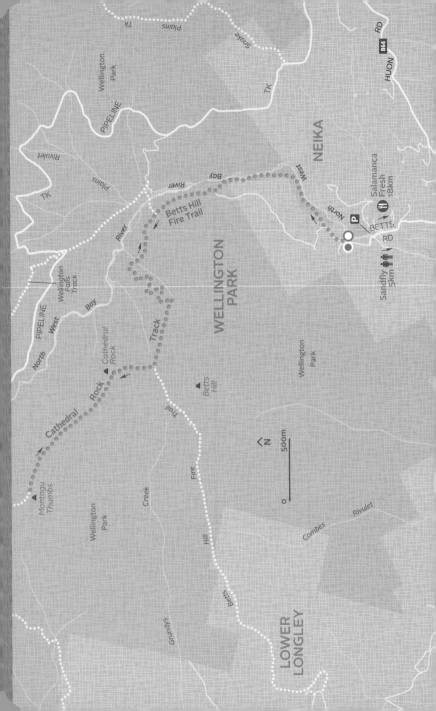

# CATHEDRAL ROCK AND MONTAGU THUMBS
## WELLINGTON PARK

104

Challenging hike and scramble along fire trails and walking tracks through eucalyptus and rainforest to rocky dolerite peaks with expansive views.

Gather together a picnic of Tassie produce from Salamanca Fresh (190 Davey St), such as Tongola goat cheese, Ziggy's smoked meats and locally grown fruit. About a kilometre along Betts Rd, you'll cross North West Bay River and there's a place to park just past the bridge. Walk up Betts Rd onto a private property and, when the main road heads off to the left, take the walking track to the right to follow the river upstream for about 100m. The track then diverts away from the river to join Betts Hill Fire Trail and it's from this point that the calf workout really begins. To Cathedral Rock it's a rise of nearly 900m in altitude from where you first began. The steepest part is the final scramble to the summit of Cathedral Rock itself, and then it's only another 100m up to Montagu Thumbs at a less extreme gradient. The views along the way and from the top of the Rock and the Thumbs render your efforts completely worthwhile.

**Location**
19km south-west from Hobart

**Distance**
11.5km return

**Grade**
Hard

**Ideal season**
Autumn

**Notes**
No dogs
Track unsealed
Be prepared for extreme changes in weather
Don't walk in wet weather or on fire ban days

Photo: Cathedral Rock
© Roger Wong

Hobart

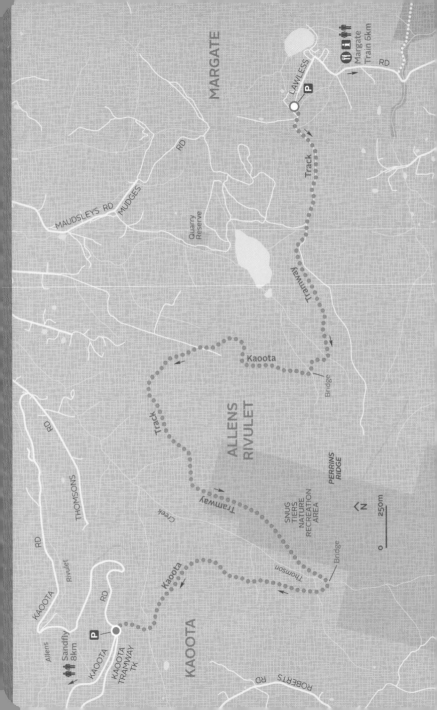

# KAOOTA TRAMWAY
## ALLENS RIVULET/KAOOTA

Gently graded walk along a historic tramway route through dry eucalyptus bushland and rainforest up to a view across the channel. Although this 1906 tramway line was dismantled in 1922, you may notice remnants of decayed infrastructure and coal spills. Watch for snakes on the track in warmer weather.

Climb aboard Tassie's last passenger train, which is now off the rails and serving up all-day pancakes in its rear carriages. Deciding between sweet and savoury could be tricky, but the bacon and maple syrup stack solves the dilemma. It was here in Margate that Kaoota's coal was shipped off from the jetty after being trundled 20km downhill on a two-foot gauge railway. Follow signs to the tramway track on Lawless Rd and park on the roadside. The steep start is not indicative of the main track, which levels out into a mild uphill climb towards Kaoota. The dry sclerophyll bushland eventually gives way to moist rainforest where quaint bridges have been constructed over squelchy creeks. Seats with sweeping views back to the water await you at the end of the track.

**Location**
30km south-west from Hobart

**Distance**
12.6km return

**Grade**
Medium

**Ideal Season**
Winter

**Notes**
No dogs
Track unsealed
Do not walk on fire ban days

Photo: Kaoota tramway track
© Elspeth Callender

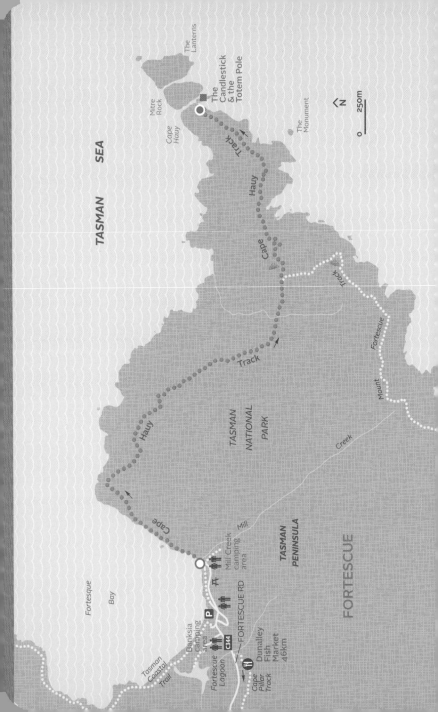

# CAPE HAUY
## TASMAN NATIONAL PARK

Coastal walk from a sheltered bay of the Tasman Peninsula up to heathland and exposed sea cliffs.

Leave the car at Fortescue Bay and find the start of the track near the boat ramp beside Mill Creek. Here, a seaside timber mill once operated. The narrow trail leads you along the coast before rising up onto a ridge of dry sclerophyll forest and past a stand of the rare Oyster Bay pine. The turnoff to Cape Hauy from this main track is clearly signposted and it's a steep hike down onto the wild and woolly saddle of the cape, vegetated mainly with coastal heath. Find safe places to lie on your belly and gaze down the length of some of the highest sea cliffs in Australia. A small track also leads to views of the Candlestick and the Totem Pole – both magnificent dolerite spires. Back at Fortescue Bay, brave a dip while you're still warm from walking. On the drive home, stop for a tasty feed at Dunalley Fish Market (11 Fulham Rd).

**106**

**Location**
97km south-east
from Hobart

**Distance**
10km return

**Grade**
Medium

**Ideal Season**
Winter

**Notes**
No dogs
Track unsealed
Do not walk on
fire ban days

Hobart

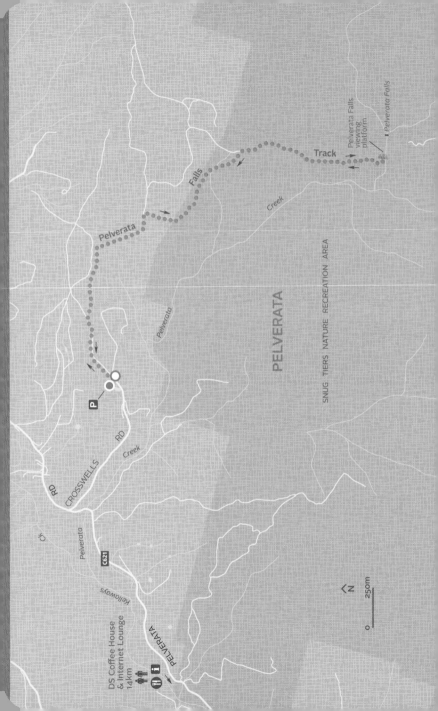

# PELVERATA FALLS
## HUON VALLEY

Peaceful walk past open pastures into dry eucalyptus bushland and rainforest with a noisy waterfall finale.

Stop off in Huonville for coffee and cake at DS Coffee House and Internet Lounge (12 Main Rd). A rich agricultural area, the Huon Valley was first settled by Europeans in the 1840s and many descendants continue to work the land. From Pelverata, follow the walking track past a typical Tasmanian scene of makeshift dwellings built on lush paddocks overlooking amazing views. Keeping to the main route, which veers right, enter the eucalyptus-dominated bushland with its tall trees and isolated pockets of rainforest. The ancient scree slope, appearing at first glance to be a rockslide that just happened, takes a little extra coordination to traverse. Local wildlife will show you how the rock-hopping is done. The narrow track soon brings you to a viewing platform that looks out onto Pelverata Falls where water will be thundering 80m down the sheer cliff-face (or dribbling depending on the season). Return to Hobart the scenic way through Kaoota.

107

**Location**
52km south-west
from Hobart

**Distance**
7km return

**Grade**
Medium

**Ideal Season**
Winter

**Notes**
No dogs
Track unsealed
Watch out
for snakes on
the track in
warmer weather

Hobart

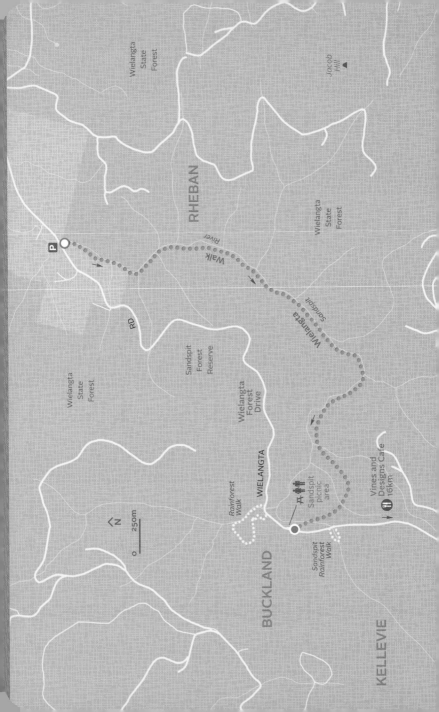

# WIELANGTA FOREST
## SANDSPIT FOREST RESERVE

Riverside walk from abandoned logging town through blue gum eucalypt production forest and pockets of cool temperate rainforest. The track follows one of the old tramway routes alongside the tree fern-lined Sandspit River. Wear long trousers and sleeves, as native cutting grass overhangs the track.

Park at the sign for the Wielangta forest walk and cross the road to where the narrow track begins. In the early 1900s, this was the site of a logging town called Wielangta, although you'll have to look closely for remnants of what was, at its height, a settlement of 100 people. Follow the old tramway route, initially alongside the Sandspit River. There's a bit of rock-hopping to do across the river and rough bridge crossings. Keep an eye out for spotted-tail quoll and eastern barred bandicoot within the blue gum forest and rainforest. After an uphill climb through grassy clearings and stands of saplings, you'll emerge at a barbecue area in Sandspit Forest Reserve. Stop in at Vines and Designs cafe at the Copping Museum (2217 Arthur Hwy) for great all-day breakfasts, where they throw in a generous dose of local quirk for free.

**108**

**Location**
78km north-east
from Hobart

**Distance**
7km return

**Grade**
Medium

**Ideal Season**
~ Winter

**Notes**
Dogs permitted
Track unsealed
Do not walk on
fire ban day

Hobart

# LABILLARDIERE PENINSULA
## SOUTH BRUNY NATIONAL PARK

109

Wild coastal circuit of ever-changing views across native heathland, through eucalyptus woodland and along secluded beaches.

Nourish yourself for the long walk ahead with coffee and sweet baked treats at Bruny Island Cheese Company (1807 Bruny Island Main Rd). Choose a favourite cheese from the tasters and grab a wood-fired sourdough for your picnic lunch. Drive on to Cape Bruny and park at the campground near the end of Old Jetty Rd, following the walking track clockwise for the best views. As you hike up out of the eucalypt forest into open coastal heathland, keep an eye out for swift parrots and endangered forty-spotted pardalotes. There's never a dull moment on this progressively narrowing track, which changes as constantly as the Tasmanian weather. As you round the tip near Partridge Island, views of dolerite sea cliffs and stony beaches on the west side are replaced by swimmable sandy beaches, ferny glades and eucalyptus woodland. Picnic on Butlers Beach gazing north across the channel towards 'mainland' Tasmania. The track re-enters the campground at Lighthouse Jetty Beach.

**Location**
92km south from Hobart

**Distance**
15km circuit

**Grade**
Medium

**Ideal Season**
Spring

**Notes**
No dogs
Track unsealed
Do not walk on fire ban days
Catch ferry from Kettering to Bruny Island
Keep an eye out for snakes across the track

Hobart

Photo: Cape Bruny Lighthouse
© Tourism Tasmania, Keith Diamond

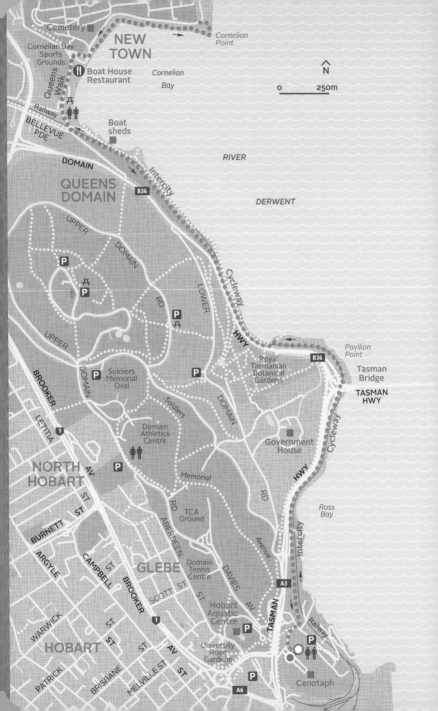

Cemetery

NEW
TOWN

Cornelian
Point

Cornelian Bay
Sports
Grounds

Queens Walk

Boat House
Restaurant

Cornelian
Bay

N

0        250m

Railway

BELLEVUE
PDE

Boat
sheds

RIVER

DOMAIN

QUEENS
DOMAIN

Intercity

B36

DERWENT

UPPER

DOMAIN

P

P

RD

UPPER

P

Cycleway

LOWER

HWY

P

Royal
Tasmanian
Botanical
Gardens

B36

Pavilion
Point

Tasman
Bridge

DOMAIN

P

TASMAN
HWY

BROOKER

DOMAIN

Soldiers Memorial Oval

Soldiers

Cycleway

LETITIA

1

Domain
Athletics
Centre

Government
House

NORTH
HOBART

P

Memorial

HWY

Ross
Bay

ST

RD

Intercity

BURNETT

ARGYLE

ST

CAMPBELL

ABERDEEN

RD

TCA
Ground

DAVIES

A3

ST

BROOKER

SCOTT

GLEBE

Domain
Tennis
Centre

AV

ST

WARWICK

HOBART

ST

ST

ST

AV

MELVILLE ST

Hobart
Aquatic
Centre

P

University
Rose
Gardens

TASMAN

Railway

P

P

Cenotaph

PATRICK

BRISBANE

ST

A6

1

# THE CENOTAPH TO CORNELIAN POINT

## CORNELIAN BAY

Easy riverside walk on a paved footpath, following the railway line, then onto an unsealed bushland track.

Begin at the Hobart Cenotaph – an Art Deco version of an Egyptian Obelisk – perched on the edge of Queens Domain with views of the city and River Derwent. Close by is the start of the Intercity Cycleway linking Hobart and Glenorchy, which is for both pedestrians and cyclists. Under the Tasman Bridge, turn right across the railway tracks and follow the signs to Cornelian Bay where you can make a beeline for the cafe and kiosk connected to the Boat House Restaurant (Queens Walk). Grab a takeaway coffee and macaron to have on Cornelian Bay Beach, or stay for chowder with ciabatta. Continue along the shoreline to a track leading into the bush that takes you all the way to Cornelian Point then circles back as a sealed road. On the way back to the Intercity Cycleway, it's well worth detouring to the boat sheds.

**Location**
200m east from Hobart

**Distance**
9km return

**Grade**
Easy

**Ideal Season**
Spring

**Notes**
Dogs permitted
Track sealed and unsealed
Watch out for trains

Hobart

Photo: Cornelian Bay
© Lynden Leppard

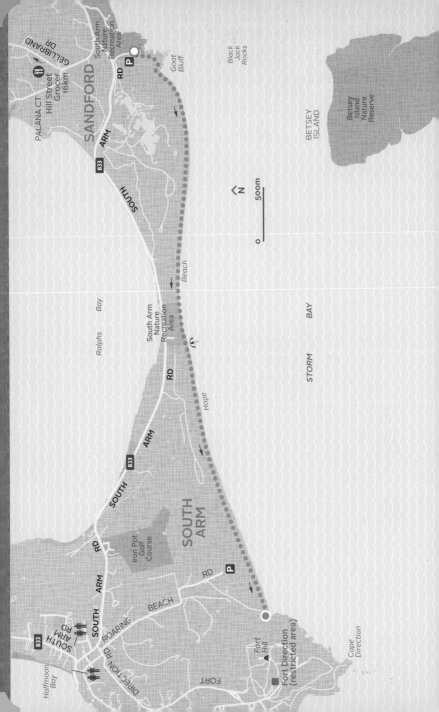

# HOPE BEACH
## SOUTH ARM

Beach walk along an exposed south-facing coastline with views out to the ocean and nearby island.

Hobart's eastern shore now has its own Hill St Grocer (528 South Arm Rd, Lauderdale) so gather together a gourmet picnic lunch on the way past. After passing Gellibrand Dr (on the right), take the next left off South Arm Rd and park at the end. This headland is Goat Bluff, though it is referred to by locals and surfers as the Wedge. Hope Beach is also known as Roaring, and its west access road, Roaring Beach Rd, is referred to as RSL's. At this part of South Arm, the River Derwent ends and Storm Bay begins, and it really feels that way; this high energy surfing beach is completely exposed to southerly swells and Antarctic winds, making it ideal for beachcombing as all sort of things wash up. About a kilometre offshore is the beguiling Betsey Island and, beside it, a lighthouse stands on a rock shelf like a baby's birthday candle. Walk towards Cape Direction until the sand runs out then find a sheltered spot to enjoy your food.

**111**

**Location**
34km south-east from Hobart

**Distance**
10km return

**Grade**
Medium

**Ideal Season**
Spring

**Notes**
Dogs permitted
Track unsealed
Multiple rips and no beach patrol; swimming not advised

Photo: Hope Beach
© Ben Short

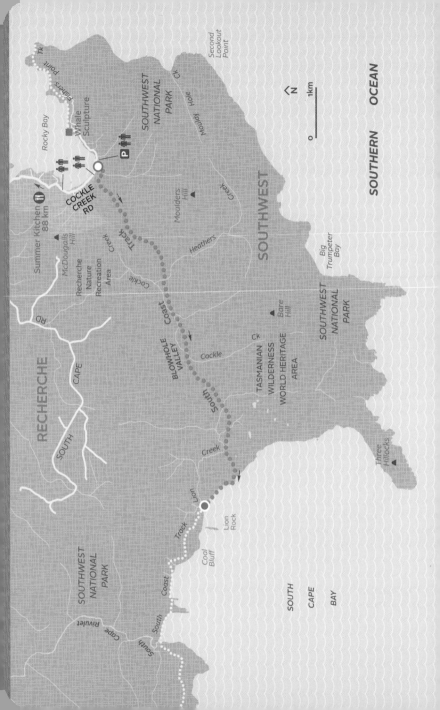

# SOUTH CAPE BAY
## SOUTHWEST NATIONAL PARK

A taste of the famous South Coast Track through various types of vegetation with a beach walk at the end. There's a lot of raised duckboard on this iconic track, which protects plants from walkers and walkers from mud. This route sees a lot of rainfall (an average of 212 days per annum), and passes through eucalyptus bushland, ferny gullies, open grasslands and mossy forest.

Summer Kitchen produces some of Hobart's best-loved bread and has a cafe in the Huon Valley (21 Marguerite St, Ranelagh), which is an ideal place to stop for a morning meal on your way south. The track begins near the carpark at Cockle Creek, which is at the southern end of Recherche Bay. The traditional owners of the area – the Lyluequonny people – camped and traded along the bay's sheltered coastline through summer and autumn, living on seal, abalone, crayfish, mussel, swan and muttonbird. Before reaching the coast, the track crosses Lion Creek for the first time. The view soon opens up to dark shale cliffs and the magnificent Southern Ocean. Walk the beach with Lion Island in view until you reach Lion Creek – the second crossing of it – where it's time to turn around.

Location
121km south-west
from Hobart

Distance
17km return

Grade
Medium

Ideal Season
Spring

Notes
No dogs
Track unsealed
Be prepared for
extreme weather
changes

Hobart

# INDEX

# ACKNOWLEDGEMENTS

The publisher would like to acknowledge the following individuals and organisations:

Commissioning editor
Melissa Krafchek

Editor
Geraldine Corridon

Design and art direction
Viola Design, Anna Carlile

Writers
Fleur Bainger, Elspeth Callender, Quentin Chester, Oliver Driscoll, Liz Ginis

Research (Melbourne)
Diana Carlile

Cartography
Bruce McGurty, Emily Maffei, Claire Johnston

Index
Max McMaster

Pre-press
Splitting Image

Cover photography credits
Snowgums, Tasmania © Rob Blakers, Getty Images
Fern © Rob Blackburn, Tourism Victoria
Coffee © Glen Murphy

Explore Australia Publishing Pty Ltd
Ground Floor, Building 1, 658 Church Street, Richmond, VIC 3121

Explore Australia Publishing Pty Ltd is a division of Hardie Grant Publishing Pty Ltd

## hardie grant publishing

Published by Explore Australia Publishing Pty Ltd, 2013

Concept, maps and form © Explore Australia Publishing Pty Ltd, 2013

Text and design © Viola Design, 2013

A Cataloguing-in-Publication entry is available from the catalogue of the National Library of Australia at www.nla.gov.au

The maps in this publication incorporate data © Commonwealth of Australia (Geoscience Australia), 2006. Geoscience Australia has not evaluated the data as altered and incorporated within this publication, and therefore gives no warranty regarding accuracy, completeness, currency or suitability for any particular purpose.

Copyright imprint and currency – VAR Product and PSMA Data

"Copyright. Based on data provided under licence from PSMA Australia Limited (www.psma.com.au)".
Hydrography Data (May 2006)
Transport Data (May 2013)

Aboriginal lands, parks and reserves based on data provided under licence from the following jurisdictions:

Australian Capital Territory Parks and Reserves (2010) – ACT Planning and Land Authority

New South Wales National Parks and Wildlife Reserves (2010) – NSW Department of Environment Climate Change and Water

Victoria Parks and Conservation Reserves (2010) – Department of Sustainability and Environment, Victoria

South Australia Protected Areas - NPWS and Conservation Reserves (2010) – Department of Environment and Natural Resources

South Australia Aboriginal Freehold Land (2010) – Primary Industries and Resources, South Australia

Protected Areas of Queensland (2010) – Department of Environment and Resource Management

Queensland Aboriginal Lands (2010) – Land and Indigenous Services, Department of Environment and Resource Management

Northern Territory Aboriginal Land Trusts (2010) – Northern Territory Department of Lands and Planning (2010)

Northern Territory Parks and Reserves (2010) – Parks and Wildlife Service – Department of Natural Resources, Environment, The Arts and Sport

Western Australia Parks and Reserves, Aboriginal Lands (June 2010) – Department of Environment and Conservation

Department of Infrastructure, Energy & Resources

Parks and Wildlife Service

Disclaimer: While every care is taken to ensure the accuracy of the data within this product, the owners of the data (including the state, territory and Commonwealth governments of Australia) do not make any representations or warranties about its accuracy, reliability, completeness or suitability for any particular purpose and, to the extent permitted by law, the owners of the data disclaim all responsibility and all liability (including without limitation, liability in negligence) for all expenses, losses, damages, (including indirect or consequential damages) and costs which might be incurred as a result of the data being inaccurate or incomplete in any way and for any reason.

ISBN-13 9781741174267

10 9 8 7 6 5 4 3 2

Printed and bound in China by 1010 Printing International Ltd

The pages of this book have been printed on 100% recycled paper.

Publisher's note: Every effort has been made to ensure that the information in this book is accurate at the time of going to press. The publisher welcomes information and suggestions for correction or improvement. Email: info@exploreaustralia.net.au

Publisher's disclaimer: The publisher cannot accept responsibility for any errors or omissions. The representation on the maps of any road or track is not necessarily evidence of public right of way. The publisher cannot be held responsible for any injury, loss or damage incurred during travel. It is vital to research any proposed trip thoroughly and seek the advice of relevant state and travel organisations before you leave.

www.exploreaustralia.net.au
Follow us on Twitter: @ExploreAus
Find us on Facebook: www.facebook.com/exploreaustralia